Patriots, Pistols, and Petticoats

PATRIOTS, PISTOLS, AND PETTICOATS

SECOND EDITION

"Poor Sinful Charles Town"
during the American Revolution

Walter J. Fraser, Jr.

UNIVERSITY OF SOUTH CAROLINA PRESS

Published in Columbia, South Carolina, by the
University of South Carolina Press

Manufactured in the United States of America

09 08 07 06 05   6 5 4 3 2

Library of Congress Cataloging-in-Publication Data

Fraser, Walter J.
   Patriots, pistols and petticoats : "poor sinful Charles Town" during the American
Revolution / Walter J. Fraser. — 2nd ed.
      p.   cm.
   Includes bibliographical references.
   ISBN 0-87249-896-4
   1. Charleston (S.C.)—History—Revolution, 1775–1783. I. Title.
   F279.C457F7   1993
   975.7'91502—dc20   92-37071

Contents

Preface

The story of Charles Town during the era of the American Revolution as I researched and told it in the first edition of *Patriots, Pistols and Petticoats*, published in 1976, remains essentially the same today. Most of the information which appeared later may be found in my book *Charleston! Charleston! The History of A Southern City* (University of South Carolina Press, 1989; paperback, 1991), which recounts the history of Charleston from 1670 to the present. I have updated the bibliography by including some of the most important books and articles on Charles Town during the struggle for American independence from Great Britain that have appeared since 1976.

I appreciate the time several colleagues spent recently to read and comment on the text after the many years it has been in print. They saved the new edition from errors on one or two substantive points. I wish also to thank the University of South Carolina Press for bringing out this second edition. After I informed the director, Ken Scott, and the acquisitions manager, Warren Slesinger, that the original edition of 15,000 copies had been depleted, both thought it would be in the public interest to publish a second edition in paperback. I hope that readers will respond as eagerly as they did to the first printing of this "popular" history of Charles Town from the 1760s to the 1780s.

Preface to the First Edition

The idea for this book grew out of discussions with members of the Charleston County Bicentennial Committee soon after I was appointed its historical consultant. Executive Committee members Dr. Gordan B. Stine, Colonel D. D. Nicholson, Jr., Captain Audley McCain, and Mr. Ben Boozer quickly recognized the need for such a book. With the approach of the 200th anniversary of the American Revolution there was no single, concise account of Charles Town during the Revolutionary Era available for either townspeople or tourists. But initially the costs of publishing such a work seemed insurmountable. The Charleston County Bicentennial Committee simply lacked the financial resources. However, when officials at Westvaco learned of the need for a book about Charles Town during the Revolutionary Era, they acted promptly and generously. Westvaco demonstrated its commitment to community projects and its support for activities relating to the celebration of American independence by offering to become the "angel" of the book. I felt honored at being asked to write it.

As the bibliography attests, I am indebted to many historians for their painstaking work in editing and interpreting the diaries, letters, journals, pamphlets, and books written by lowcountry citizens and visitors of the Revolutionary Generation. Mrs. Granville T. Prior at the South Carolina Historical Society and Colonel James H. Hillard of The Citadel Library facilitated my archival research. My colleagues in The Citadel History Department kindly offered their assistance. Colonel Charles L. Anger read the manuscript and commented on it; Professor Larry H. Addington, a specialist in modern military history, shared with me his extensive knowledge of weapons, tactics, and personalities of the Revolutionary

Era; Professor Jamie W. Moore and Colonel Richard H. Hansen offered invaluable technical assistance. As he has done on other occasions, Professor W. Bland Mathis, Jr., of The Citadel English Department salvaged several convoluted sentences and saved me from some other blunders. Professor George C. Rogers, Jr., Yates Snowden Professor of History at the University of South Carolina, found time in his busy schedule of teaching and writing to read the manuscript and offer insights which had eluded me. Finally, the book is dedicated to young Thomas and young Jay and to all others who would seek to learn something of the heritage from which they sprang.

Walter J. Fraser, Jr., Ph.D.
Associate Professor, History
The Citadel

Patriots, Pistols, and Petticoats

CHAPTER I

"Poor Sinful Charles Town"

Coming in by sea to the fourth largest city in the 13 North American Colonies of Great Britain, a New Jersey merchant watched a northeast wind churn ocean swell-tops white. As the schooner approached at dawn that day in 1772, he saw "the Light House near the Charles Town Bar." The captain "fearing to fall to Seaward of the bar beat on and waiting for a Pilot boat continued to stand on till the tide suited to run over the Bar."

Apprehensive until they had cleared the town's natural defense against invasion by sea, a sand bar at the harbor's entrance, passengers aboard ships once inside the obstruction observed that "Charles Town makes a very handsome appearance. What adds greatly to the prospect is Sullivan's Island at the mouth of the Bay on the right hand, and Ashley and Cooper Rivers running on each side the Town." As their ships moved closer they could see "fine fertile looking country, well wooded with noble lofty pines and oaks forming a prospect upon the whole strikingly beautiful."

Courtesy Carolina Art Association/Gibbes Museum of Art
Charles Town's Harbor, 1762

The good natural harbor and a productive hinterland linked to the town by a network of roads and rivers had made Charles Town the importing and exporting center of the Southern Colonies. A Rhode Island merchant in town on business during the 1760's noted that "the Port has vessels entering every day from all the Islands, Europe, North America, St. Augustine, Pensacola, and Mobile." Josiah Quincy of Massachusetts upon entering the harbor in 1773 observed that "the number of shipping far surpassed all I have seen in Boston. About three hundred and fifty sail lay off the town."

The city itself was situated on the tip of a narrow peninsula laced with tidal creeks. By the early 1770's Charles Town embraced a population of approximately 12,000, of which one-half were Negro slaves. It was the seat of the Royal Governor of South Carolina, his Council, and the popularly elected Commons House of Assembly. Bay Street, lined with wholesale stores and residencies, ran parallel to the Cooper River, which bounded the city on the east. Like long fingers, wharves stretched into the Cooper which resembled a "floating market" during the fall months. It was choked with brigantines, sloops, and

Courtesy Gibbes Art Gallery, Charleston, S. C.
Another View of Charles Town's Harbor, 1760's

Courtesy The Metropolitan Museum of Art, Fletcher Fund, 1928

Gabriel Manigault

schooners from abroad and "pettiaugas" and canoes from the interior which brought the country produce to town and returned down the rivers and creeks loaded with goods ordered by the planters.

Christopher Gadsden's wharf on the Cooper was described in the early 1770's as "the most extensive of the kind ever undertaken by any one man in North America." Gadsden was a country factor who purchased products in the hinterland, delivered them to his wharf, and sold and shipped them abroad. In 1774 he described his wharf as one "at which thirty of the largest ships that can come over our bar can be loading at the same time and all float at low water with their whole loads in." Other wharves jutting into the Cooper included those of John Gaillard near the Fish Market at the end of Queen Street and one owned by Samuel Prioleau, Jr. By the mid-1770's wharf construction was underway along the Ashley River, which bounded the town on the west. The factor William Gibbes was building one of the most elaborate.

Tons of exports and imports flowed across these wharves each year. Charles Town factors like Gadsden, merchants like Gabriel Manigault, who imported wares for sale in his shops in Tradd Street, and Henry Laurens grew wealthy in the trade. They invested their profits in land. By the early 1770's Laurens owned at least eight plantations and had an annual income of 2,500 pounds sterling. He was one of the wealthiest men in the British Colonies. When Gabriel Manigault died in the early 1780's he left an estate which included 47,532 acres of land and 490 slaves, a fortune equaled by few in America.

Planters along the Ashley and Cooper Rivers and on the sea islands near Charles Town like Henry and Arthur Middleton, William Henry Drayton, and Rawlins Lowndes grew rich on the export trade of rice and indigo. By the 1760's an initial investment in slaves and land for the planting of indigo could be recouped after three or four good crops. Men of humble birth and failures in their first careers became rich during middle age by shrewd investments in land and slaves. The lowcountry Carolinian Joseph Allston was poor at 40, but at 50 he had an annual income of 6,000 pounds sterling from the exportation of rice and indigo grown on five plantations and worked by over 500 slaves. John Stuart also jumped from near bankruptcy to rich planter in a few years. He "bragged in brick" and timber of his

Courtesy Middleton Place

Arthur Middleton and Family

wealth by building a magnificent Georgian style home on Tradd Street.

Factors, merchants, and planters owned outright or jointly hundreds of vessels which plied the export-import trade routes each year. By the 1760's Gadsden had an interest in at least 5, Manigault in 6, and Henry Laurens in 12 ranging from the 10-ton coastal trading schooner *Dependence* to the 180-ton open-sea ship *Nelly*.

The names given to those vessels registered or built in Charles Town during the early eighteenth century indicate the owners' pursuit of wealth and status — *Merchants Adventure, Good Hope, Enterprize, Success,* and *Endeavour.* On the eve of the American Revolution, however, names given to vessels out of the Carolina port are indicative of the growing nationalism and desire for economic and political independence. Keels were laid for the *Fair America* and *Heart of Oak,* and after 1764 nine ships out of Charles Town were christened *Liberty.*

Courtesy the National Portrait Gallery, Smithsonian Institution, Washington, D. C.

Henry Laurens

The hazards facing the owners and masters of these trading vessels, any dozen of which could be accommodated on the deck of a modern aircraft carrier, were many. One such danger is illustrated by the cryptic notice in the *South Carolina Gazette* published in Charles Town on March 26, 1771: "Captain Edward King of the sloop *Ruth* was washed overboard in a violent storm on voyage from this port to Dominica."

Courtesy South Carolina Historical Society
Seal of Henry Laurens

Courtesy South Carolina Historical Society
Charles Town House of Henry Laurens

The holds of outward bound ships carried the lowcountry's prime export, rice, from Charles Town to colonial ports, to Barbadoes and Barcelona, to London and to Leith. During 1771, the peak year of rice exportation, 130,784 barrels went out of the port town. The need for diversification of crops, Eliza Lucas Pinckney's successful experiments with indigo growing near Charles

Town, and England's demand for a dye needed by the growing textile industry contributed to the rise of the second major lowcountry export. By 1775 over a million pounds of indigo was departing through the port annually. The mercantile policies of Great Britain which provided "price supports," a ready market, and protection by the Royal Navy helped to make men rich quickly in the lowcountry. Such items as tar, pitch, turpentine, lumber, corn, peas, potatoes, beef, pork, deerskins, tallow, tobacco, snake root, and oranges also were in great demand abroad; these left the port town by the thousands of barrels, bushels, tubs, casks, and boxes each year. These products flowed from plantation to port down the Ashley and Cooper by small boats and by wagons drawn along the network of roads leading to Charles Town.

Wealthy planters spent the cooler, fever-free months in Charles Town. During the "sickly season" they deserted the city for their plantations along the Ashley and Cooper. These country seats bore such exotic names as "Vaucluse," "Sans Souci," and "Stromboli"; "Runnymede" indicated the owner's English origins. Others were named for the nearby topography — "The Oaks," "Ashley Bluff," "Millbrook," and "Palmettos."

A visitor to George Marshall's 84-acre plantation on the Ashley about three miles from town in June, 1765, "viewed his plantation, saw his rice and indigo growing in the field, and a very beautiful orangery, and fine garden with a variety of fine vegetables." A neighboring plantation was advertised for sale. It included "a large two-story Mansion House" facing the river, a barn, kitchen, overseer's house, and slave cabins of wood. The owner advertised that "there is land sufficient to work 50 or 60 Negroes on corn, rice, and indigo for *one hundred years*." In short, the "plantation is calculated for Profit. Any person that loves profit, mixed with

Pleasure may make it the garden of the Province."
Another plantation of over 400 acres near the conflu-
ence of the Ashley River and Wappoo Creek was advertised as having "exceeding good land for indigo, a good
oven, two sets of large white oak indigo vats, and a large
pump and two sets of brick vats." Included in the sale
were "upward of FIFTY likely strong NEGROES," two
of whom were cask makers; two cooks, "one of which is
a *professed* cook; seamstresses, housewenches, washer
women and waiting-men, plantation slaves and handy
boys and girls."

The accumulation of fortunes by Ashley and Cooper
River planter-merchants through the growth and sale of
rice and indigo would have been impossible without
the toil and sweat of West Africans. It is little wonder
that one of the port town's major imports was black
slaves. From 1735-1775 more than 400 Charles Town
merchants and factors imported 1,108 separate ship-
loads of Africans. In 1765 over 7,000 blacks were
brought into Charles Town's port aboard slave ships.
Thousands of these slaves were sold in South Carolina
and thousands more in the neighboring colonies. De-
scribing the sale of imported blacks, a Charles Town
resident wrote: "They are exposed on a sort of stage,
turned about and exhibited, put up and adjudged to the
highest bidder."

Slaves performed the heavy and menial labor on the
plantations and in Charles Town. Negro women performed services as wet nurses. Infant sons and
daughters of wealthy planters and merchants "are usually suckled by Negro wenches and associate with the
Negroes for several of the first years of their lives," a
Northern-born visitor was surprised to learn. A visiting
Jerseyman was struck by the number of personal black
servants attending the gentry. Even "every child has
one accompanying it," he exclaimed.

A merchant from Jamaica who stopped in Charles Town in 1773 observed: "There are swarms of Negroes about the Town and many Mulattoes." The Jamaican had heard of "one Gentleman who professedly keeps a Mulatto Mistress." The Pennsylvania-born geographer-historian Ebenezer Hazard learned of "black dances" in Charles Town — "balls given by Negro and Mulatto women to which they invite the white gentlemen." He was informed that the Mulatto women "dress elegantly and have no small acquaintance with polite behavior." At least one Charles Town wife left her husband because of his attentions to a slave woman. On November 14, 1768, Mary Myers announced in the *South Carolina Gazette* that Mr. Myers had driven her away by "inhumanity and preferring an old Negro wench for a bedfellow."

Many of the slaves were not content with their existence. Some tried to flee from their owners. While Ebenezer Hazard was visiting near Charles Town in the 1770's, he wrote in his journal: "Saw a Negro man on the road who had run away from his master: I came up just at the instant that another Negro was tying him with a rope." Hazard noticed the slaves' white owner sitting nearby "on horseback, with a gun in his hand."

When slave revolts occurred or rumors of insurrections spread across the lowcountry, the white inhabitants were terrified. When the Pennsylvanian Hazard questioned lowcountry persons as to why Negro slaves were sometimes treated harshly, he was told "that it is necessary in order to break their spirits, and thereby prevent insurrection."

The Northern-born Hazard came to hold a low opinion of slavery. He discovered that lowcountry Carolinians justified keeping Negroes in servitude because "they were born on purpose to be slaves." Another justification was "that white people could not endure the fatigues [of] labor in the Southern states." However, Hazard believed that this was only "begging the question." He thought that one of the "true causes" of enslaving Negroes was that "the expense of Negroes will amount to a less sum than hiring of white persons would." The Northern native also believed that the basis for keeping Negroes in bondage was partly psychological. It inflated the ego and status of white men of all classes.

Besides serving as common laborers, slaves were employed as skilled craftsmen in Charles Town shops. Sometimes their owners hired them out by the day, week, or job. But this "jobbing out" often created a scarcity of jobs for other skilled white artisans in Charles Town. These white craftsmen formed a "middling" social class between the wealthy merchant, planter, and professional man at the top of the social ladder and the indentured white servant and Negro at the bottom.

In addition to the slaves, hundreds of other items were imported for sale. During the 1760's the merchant James McCall advertised in the Charles Town papers items he imported from Bristol: saws, iron pots, bullets, gunpowder, window glass, nails, canvas, drugs, Bird Fountains, Hearth-tiles, bridles and whips, bowls, decanters, tea and coffee pots, candlesticks, ale, Gloucestershire cheese, candy, gloves, shoes, "handsome flowered silks," "silk umbrelloes," ribbons, India bordered chintz, and "a great variety of USEFUL ARTICLES" could be bought "at his store in Tradd Street, remarkable cheap, especially for CASH."

Charles Town artisans, the "middling class," often purchased in quantity from merchants like McCall and Gabriel Manigault. The tailors of the town bought cloth to outfit local dandies in their velvet capes and gold-buttoned coats. Shoemakers like John and Simon Berwick, however, kept a tanyard which provided the leather for their craft. In their Charles Town shoe shop they sold "Negro Shoes" as well as finer quality shoes for men, women, and children. Working closely with the tanners and cordwainers were the numerous saddlers in the town. Barrelmaking was a particularly important occupation, given the extensive export trade. Daniel Saylor maintained a cooperage factory near the wharves. Barrelmaker Gabriel Guignard became wealthy at his craft. In the bustling port town hundreds of carpenters, painters, glaziers, sail and rope makers were engaged in the building, repair, and alteration of sailing vessels. Among the craftsmen were the tinsmiths who made "fire-buckets," covered roofs, and lit the street lamps of the town. There were wigmakers, weavers, seamstresses, and barbers. Bakers made fancy pastry as well as "ships bread" or hardtack, tobacconists kept "Smoking Shops" in the English style, and brewers produced beer.

Edmund Egan was perhaps Charles Town's most successful brewer-businessman before the Revolution. By 1772 he had erected a "large and expensive Malt house" and adopted the slogan "Let the beer justify itself." The *South Carolina Gazette* praised his product as "superior to most that is usually imported from the Northern Colonies."

In the Carolina port town as in England it was customary for the wife of a shopkeeper or artisan to work as her husband's partner and at his death continue the business alone. Women in the town also opened businesses independent of their husbands' trades. Even single women launched commercial ventures. Between 1760 and 1775 there were at least 36 proprietresses of shops in Charles Town.

Frances Swallow not only ran a chic women's fashion shop; when her husband died, she opened a tavern to support herself and her six children. When Agnes Lind, the proprietress of a millinery business, died in October, 1766, her husband Thomas Lind advertised for an assistant. Miss Katherine Smith applied, was accepted, and in December Thomas married Katherine! She ran the business for five years until Thomas died. Nine months later Katherine Lind married William Bower, a watchmaker. Now Katherine Bower advertised for sale at her millinery shop "the fourth corner of Tradd Street next the Bay" such items as "fashionable caps," lace, satin, ribbons, fans, gloves, needles, and beads. All could be purchased "on the lowest TERMS."

Women staymakers, handkerchief, bonnet, and ruffle makers kept shops. In 1769 Mary Drysdell opened a business of "starching, washing and scouring silk stockings, and cleaning Silks from any spots of Grease." The same year Margaret Nelson opened a pastry shop offering for sale plum cakes, custards, puddings, tarts, marmalade, and potted beef.

Through the Charles Town newspapers, women also advertised as upholsterers, crockery menders, livery stable keepers, shipwrights, barbers, and butchers. At least one lady ran an establishment which employed practitioners of one of the most ancient occupations. In 1764 a Grand Jury indicted "Mary M'Dowell [of] Pinckney's Street for keeping a most notorious brothel for Lewd Women."

Included among the dozens of industrial artists of the town in the 1770's were cabinetmakers, silversmiths, engravers, blacksmiths, painters, and builders. Competition was so keen among cabinetmakers that Richard Magrath had to defend himself in the *Gazette* from slurs on his work by some "wretch." Magrath urged his customers to "pay no regard to the words of such a low groveling Fellow, pregnant with impudence, Ignorance, and Falsehoods." Perhaps the most popular cabinetmaker was Thomas Elfe. He produced 1,500 pieces of furniture—chests, chairs, and sofas—between 1768 and 1775. Like the merchants and planters, he too invested in land and slaves. At Elfe's death his heirs inherited a considerable estate. The Charles Town cabinetmakers followed the styles of the English masters—Sheraton, Hepplewhite, Chippendale, and Adam—but they frequently added rice ears and leaves to their pieces in homage to the staple of the lowcountry. Thus, while the people of the new world were imitating the English styles, their work was influenced by their environment.

The demands of the new world on the industrial artists made versatility a virtue. Blacksmiths like William Johnson, James Lingard, and John Cleaton shod horses, erected lightning rods, did scroll or plain work on railings for staircases, and advertised that they did "many other branches that are manufactured in iron too tedious to enumerate."

George Flagg, Benjamin Hawes, John and Hamilton Stevenson, Charles Town portrait painters, taught drawing to support themselves. The most highly respected of the town's pre-revolutionary painters was Jeremiah Theus. The colors he used in portraying the lowcountry elite were excellent. They remain so to this day by comparison to the colors used in portraits done by his contemporaries.

The rapid accumulation of wealth by merchants and planters and their desire to "brag in brick" in both private and public structures kept Charles Town's artisan builders busy. During the 1760's numerous buildings and dwellings were being erected along Bay,

Tradd, Meeting, King, Broad, and Boundary Streets and in the first suburbs, Ansonborough, Harleston Village, and White Point. A Northern merchant in the town in 1764 wrote: "One cannot go anywhere where one does not see new buildings and large and small houses started, half finished, and almost finished. To me who comes from poor humble Rhode Island, it seems a new world." A few year later, Peter Timothy, editor of the *Gazette*, told his friend Benjamin Franklin: "Private and public works are everywhere carrying on with Spirit."

Architects like Samuel Cardy, housewrights John and Peter Horlbeck, Timothy Crosby, Ezra Waite, Humphrey Sommers, Daniel Cannon, and the carver Thomas Bernard accumulated modest wealth from the demands for design and construction. Assisting these independent artisans in the building trades were black slaves and indentured white servants. The latter usually pledged their services for a four- to seven-year period in return for passage to America. Indentured white laborers, like the Negro slave, sometimes ran away. So disgusted was the Charles Town artisan Edward Weyman with one of his persistent runaways that he offered those who apprehended and returned him the "reward of Two Large Hand Fulls of Pine Shavings for their trouble."

The white indentures after completing their periods of servitude often became independent businessmen. Abraham Daphne, carpenter, advertised in the *Gazette* that he had finished his period of indenture and was now ready "to undertake any work in his business at reasonable prices." Daniel Cannon, another carpenter who began as an indentured servant in Charles Town, became an independent artisan and by investing his profits from the building trade in land retired a wealthy man. In less than a generation men sometimes moved from near the bottom of the social ladder to the top.

The structures designed and built by Charles Town architects, carpenters, bricklayers, and their assistants elicited a variety of comments from visitors. The private dwellings along Broad and Meeting Streets were described as "large, handsome, modern built Brick Houses." Some were "of brick inside and plaistered over on the outside" while others were done "entirely of wood." Usually brick, cypress, and yellow pine went into the construction. By 1774 "all White Point [was] almost covered with Houses, many of them very elegant." The homes of William Gibbes, Thomas Savage, and Miles Brewton were among these houses, and they still stand today.

Shortly after the completion of the home of the wealthy merchant Miles Brewton, a dinner guest described the interior of the dwelling as having "the grandest hall I ever beheld." At the windows he saw "azure blue satin curtains," wallpaper of "rich blue with gilt, most ele-

Courtesy South Carolina Historical Society

Miles Brewton House

gant pictures, and excessive grand and costly looking glasses."

A first consideration of the lowcountry builders was the torrid heat of the summers. A German-born medical doctor noted that generally the homes of Charles Town had "airy and cool rooms, spacious yards and gardens." The kitchens were "always placed in a separate building to avoid the heat and the danger of fire." A Frenchman visiting Charles Town observed that "everything peculiar to the buildings of this place is formed to moderate the excessive heat. The windows are open and the doors pass through both sides of the houses. Every endeavour is used to refresh within with fresh air." Piazzas were added "to shelter the houses from the force of the sun's rays." The visitor believed that the inhabitants of the town "vie with one another, not who shall have the finest, but who the coolest house."

The public structures raised by Charles Town builders in the 1760's and early 1770's also were striking monuments to the growing wealth of the lowcountry. Shortly after the Commons House of Assembly divided the town into two parishes, St. Philip's and St. Michael's, plans were laid to begin construction of a church in the latter parish to rival the one in the former. By December, 1762, St. Michael's Church had been erected on the southeast corner of Broad and Meeting Streets opposite the newly built State House on the northwest corner. The similarly designed County Court House stands there today. The steeple of the church soared above the rooftops of its parish houses and remains one of the highest points in the city.

In 1767 contracts were awarded to builders William Rigby Naylor and James Brown to construct a new Watch House on the southwest corner of Broad and Meeting. Here were to be located the offices of the

The Exchange Building

county comptroller, the treasurer, and the powder-receiver. On the northeast corner of Meeting and Broad stood the Beef Market where one could purchase meat from sunrise to sunset six days a week. During the same year a contract was given to Peter and John Horlbeck to construct the Exchange at the foot of Charles Town's principal thoroughfare, Broad Street. Built in the grand Palladian style, the structure was completed by the fall of 1771 and thought to be one of the sights in America.

For those arriving at Charles Town by sea, the Exchange Building was the formal entrance to the town. At the lower level they could transact customs business; the entrance level was an open arcade, while the upper level or Great Hall was used for dancing assemblies and civic meetings.

The beauty and dignity of Charles Town's public edifices, the private homes overlooking wide streets with well-attended gardens, prompted praise from visitors in the 1770's. Seeing Charles Town for the first time, the Rhode Islander Elkanah Watson exclaimed: "Perhaps no city of America exhibits, in proportion to its size, so much splendor and style."

Not noted for their architectural beauty, but rather for their choice liquors and "good larders in season," were Charles Town's taverns and inns. Patronized by the local citizens, persons stopping in town for amusement, shopping, or business, and populated by the gentlemen from the countryside during sessions of the courts and Assembly, the public taverns of the town were kinds of community centers. Charles Shepheard's Tavern at the northeast corner of Broad and Church Streets, today the site of a bank, and Robert Dillon's, later William Holliday's, establishment on Queen Street were two of the most popular during the 1760's and 1770's. Several women also kept taverns during this period. Tavern hostess Elizabeth Carne offered "entertainment for Man and Horse" at her Broad Street establishment; Ann Hawes "at the sign of the Bacchus" advertised "the best [in] Liquors and Relishes."

While patrons downed such rum-based drinks as "slings," "flipps," and "toddies," or wine, molasses and persimmon beer, ate salted fish, wild-game, sweet-meats, rice-flour puddings, and nuts, they could argue politics, play dice, cards, billiards, watch cockfights and occasionally a duel. The most celebrated incident involving the *code duello* occurred at Holliday's Tavern on August 15, 1771. At about eight in the evening, Dr. John Haly and Peter De Lancey, both "heated with liquor," arranged to meet at the tavern. Here they faced each other at point-blank range and fired simultaneously. Shot in the chest, De Lancey died instantly while Haly escaped unscathed. Murder charges were brought against the latter, but he was acquitted when the court accepted the argument that De Lancey's death resulted from duelling wounds.

Civic leaders sometimes agonized over the baneful influences of the taverns on the lower classes. In 1762 the Assembly enacted a law levying a fine of 20 shillings on any apprentice, laborer, or servant found gaming at a place which sold liquor. A few years later a committee appointed by the Assembly to investigate the cause for the sharp increase in taxes for relief of the indigent concluded that a central factor was the "superabundance of licensed taverns & tipling houses within & near Charles Town." The committee believed that repeated visitations to these public houses by many of the lower classes had led to the "ruin of their health" and plunged them into poverty.

Although the "better sort" in Charles Town might occasionally worry over the dissipation among the lower orders, merchants and planters themselves vigorously pursued pleasure and amusements, the companions of great wealth and leisure. In expensive carriages, planters and their families crowded the roads leading to Charles Town at the beginning of the annual social season. Here they dove into a social whirl lasting from January to the early spring. The country elite mingled with the town merchants at public taverns and private clubs. At the Monday Night Club, the Smoking Club, the Hellfire Club, the Friday Night Club, or at the Jockey Club races, "cards, dice, the bottle and horses engross prodigious portions of time and attention," a Northern visitor to Charles Town observed. What conversations there were turned on "land, negroes, and rice." Sometimes they went to their hunt clubs where after the morning chase, the afternoons were "spent very merry, after killing foxes."

To pacify their wives and daughters who sometimes complained of neglect due to the "parties of pleasure" for gentlemen only, the wealthy families of both countryside and town attended balls, concerts, and the theatre during the annual social season.

The vivacious Eliza Wilkinson wrote of her excitement in preparing for a Charles Town ball in the 1760's: "The important day arrived, and there was such powdering! and frizzing and curling! and dressing." Mixing with the other "powdered Beau and Belles" at the ball, Eliza found "the Musick played sweetly, so sweetly that I could not keep my feet still." And she danced away the "happy hours." Even politics was subordinated to dancing. During the social season of 1763, Henry Laurens disgustedly noted that sessions of the Legislature were shortened "in favor of the ball."

The love of dancing and music in the lowcountry was unrivaled in the rest of America. Even though well-to-do planters' daughters daily faced an exhausting list of responsibilities in overseeing the work of household slaves and conducting schools for the Negro children, they found time for music. The sprightly Eliza Lucas, later Pinckney, practiced music in the morning and evening and met weekly with her "music master."

It is not surprising that the first musical society founded in America, the St. Cecilia Society, was organized in Charles Town. Attending a concert given by the Society during the social season of 1773, Josiah Quincy found "the musick good: the two bass-violas and French horns were grand." The very proper Bostonian could not help but compare the 250 ladies he saw there with the ladies of Massachusetts. The Charles Town ladies, Quincy observed, "in loftiness of headdress stoop to the daughters of the North: in richness and elegance of dress surpass them." During the performance he found the Charles Town ladies less reserved than Boston ladies while "in noise and flirtations after the music is over pretty much on the par." Comparing the beauty of the locals with those of Boston, Quincy favored the looks of the ladies of his native ground.

A Frenchman visiting Charles Town about the same time disagreed with the Bostonian. He found the Carolina women lively, "interesting and agreeable." A native Carolinian observed that the ladies of Charles Town were "genteel and slender," free and unaffected in their manner. An English visitor differed sharply. Mixing with the elite of the town and country at balls, concerts, and the theatre, he remarked that with few exceptions "the ladies are not tolerably handsome." Most, he wrote, "have Pale Sickish Languid Complections and are commonly illshaped, their Shoulders seeming to have a longing desire to rise high enough to hide their ears." In their conversation, the Englishman discovered, the ladies "have a disagreeable drawling way of speaking." A Virginian was surprised to discover that lowcountry gentlewomen "talk like Negroes."

Plays were performed more frequently in Charles Town than in any of the other Colonies, and the theatre was another highlight of the social season. When David Douglass and his famous traveling troupe, the American Company of Comedians, performed at the newly built theatre on Queen Street during the 1763-1764 season, Mrs. Ann Manigault was in constant attendance. On December 22 she wrote in her diary: "To the play — 'The Mourning Bride' "; she attended the theatre on the evenings of January 13, February 3, 13, 24, and 27; on March 19 she wrote: "to the play — 'The Jealous Wife' " and "ditto" she entered on March 29; in April she went to the theatre twice seeing *The Mourning Bride* again and *Romeo and Juliet.* On May 2 she saw *King Lear.* It appears that only illness prevented her from attending every performance during the season.

Perhaps the most "brilliant" and "gayest" season in the history of the colonial theatre occurred in Charles Town during the winter of 1773-1774. Seventy-seven different plays were performed at a newly built structure on Church Street. Even the *New York Gazette* raved about the new theatre. "It is elegantly furnished," the Northern paper reported, and is regarded as "the most commodious on the continent." On opening night the scenes, dresses, music, and "disposition of the lights contributed to the satisfaction of the audience who expressed the highest approbation of their entertainment."

It is small wonder that the pleasure-pursuing and amusement-seeking social elite of Charles Town neglected religion. Outward appearance would seem to suggest that the citizens were a very religious people. Anglicanism, the established religion supported by public taxation, was represented by St. Philip's and St. Michael's Churches; there were six "meeting houses" — an Independent, Presbyterian, French Huguenot, Lutheran, and two Baptist; an "assembly house" for Quakers was located on King Street as was Beth Elohim, the first Jewish congregation in Charles Town. However, clergy and visiting laity alike were surprised at the casual approach to religion and in some cases even outright immorality among the inhabitants of the town.

Coming from Massachusetts where his Puritan ances-
tors took religion quite seriously, Josiah Quincy was
surprised to see so "very few present" when he attended
services at St. Philip's. He was equally surprised to hear
a sermon of less than 20 minutes and to "see gentlemen
conversing together in prayer as well as sermon-time."
Quincy believed that "the state of religion here is re-
pugnant to the ordinances and institutions of Jesus
Christ." One Anglican rector was outraged by Charles
Town's "fashionable principles of libertinism and in-
fidelity." Another was upset when he discovered that
most of the brides he joined in holy wedlock were pregnant. In 1774 the pastor of the Huguenot Church bemoaned the "great decay and almost utter dissolution"
of his congregation. The Baptist divine, the Reverend
Oliver Hart, frequently fretted over "poor sinful Charles
Town."

With the exception of a few well-to-do physicians, merchants, and planters, an indifference to intellectual pur-
suits also prevailed in Charles Town.

The semi-tropical climate, the nearby rice fields and
swamps which were breeding grounds for swarms of
mosquitoes, made Charles Town an exciting, hazard-
ous, but profitable place for medical practitioners and
researchers alike. Besides treating such perennial diseases like cholera, pleurisy, and the gout, physicians
were kept busy during the "sickly season" when
epidemics of whooping cough, measles, various fevers,
and the dreaded smallpox swept through the city.
Common opinion had it that "Carolina is in the spring a
paradise, in the summer a hell, and in the Autumn a
hospital." Writing to a young student who nearly had
completed his medical studies abroad, Henry Laurens
advised him to return to Charles Town in August: "and

you will probably arrive at a Season which unfortunately for us poor Mortals is generally a good one for the Gentlemen of your profession."

As their eighteenth century counterparts in England, Charles Town doctors prescribed bleeding and sweating and vomit-inducing concoctions for their patients. Citizens believed that some doctors carried off more persons than did diseases. No doubt quacks abounded. Unsuccessfully Charles Town physicians attempted to license all medical men to prevent such abuses which one inhabitant complained of—those "doctors" who "made an Apothecary shop of my Stomach."

Young Peter Fayssoux who returned to Charles Town after receiving his medical degree from Edinburgh University in 1769 found to his disgust that "it is sufficient for a man to call himself a Doctor, & he immediately becomes one, & finds fools to employ him." However, among the 35 to 40 physicians in Charles Town, Fayssoux also found "respectable names, Men of Letters & candour." These were men like John Moultrie, Lionel Chalmers, Alexander Garden, and William Loocock.

Despite opposition from the townspeople, Dr. Loocock championed inoculation against smallpox during epidemics in the 1760's. He founded a hospital on Broad Street in 1762. Physicians also promoted the establishment of a "Pest House" on Sullivan's Island for the quarantining of those persons showing signs of contagious diseases. In 1770, long before the germ theory of disease was known, Dr. Lionel Chalmers of Charles Town worried over the unpaved, "dusty," "dirty" streets. He was concerned about the "many narrow lanes and alleys" which "may prove a nursery for diseases." His research and observations led to the publication in London in the 1770's of a two-volume work on weather and disease. The book was one of the major

American contributions to general medicine during the colonial period.

The work of physician and naturalist Alexander Garden of Charles Town was internationally recognized. The Swedish naturalist Linnaeus complimented Garden by naming one of his new plant discoveries the gardenia. Soon afterwards Dr. Lewis Mottet's jealousy of this recognition of Garden emerged when Mottet announced that he too had discovered a beautiful native plant. He planned to name it "Lucia," after his cook Lucy.

Sometimes the veneration in which a few physicians of the town were held emerged only at their death. Legend has it that when the obstetrician Dr. John Moultrie, Sr., died in 1771, Charles Town ladies were plunged into mourning.

These few lowcountry scientists and physicians also helped provide the intellectual leadership which led to the establishment of the Library Society and the Charles Town Museum. The former established in 1748 loaned books to the general public and sponsored scientific experiments. The natural history museum organized in 1773 was the first of its kind in America.

The general prevailing intellectual indifference in the lowcountry is illustrated by the Assembly's repeated refusals to vote funds for the establishment of schools. Therefore, the only education available to the lower classes was through the few free grammar schools or charity schools supported by benevolent societies. Although there were private boarding schools in Charles Town and numerous tutors available for those who could afford them, Henry Laurens bemoaned that Carolina children had to be sent to England even "for A B C and a little Latin."

Throughout the colonial period, South Carolina had no institution of higher learning as did Boston, New York, Philadelphia, Williamsburg, and other colonial towns. The few wealthy who thought of education at all sent their children abroad. Laurens and Charles Pinckney even accompanied their sons to England for their educations.

Only the male offspring of the lowcountry gentry traveled to England for higher education, and most of these studied law. This practical education not only prepared them to practice, but prepared these elite for careers as merchants, planters, or politicians. The names of those who studied at the Inns of Court read like a who's who of the lowcountry Revolutionary generation—Arthur Middleton, Edward Rutledge, Thomas Heyward, Thomas Lynch, Charles Cotesworth and Thomas Pinckney, and John Faucherand Grimke. But as to the education they received in England, a learned visitor to Charles Town in the 1770's believed that the sons of the gentry who were sent abroad "generally attended more to fashion while there than to learning." On the eve of the Revolution, fewer than 20 lowcountry natives held college or university degrees.

Commenting on the education of the daughters of the wealthy elite who attended the expensive Charles Town boarding schools for instruction in dancing, music, French, needlework, and drawing, Ebenezer Hazard believed that "their education is scandalously neglected." An anonymous local critic agreed. Since the young ladies of the town are trained in "no professions except Music and Dancing," he wrote, they "make very agreeable Companions, but expensive wives." After consorting with the Charles Town gentry and their families in the early 1770's, Josiah Quincy wrote: "Nothing that I saw raised my conception of the mental abilities of this people."

It is not surprising that Northern contemporaries like Hazard and Quincy viewed most of the 5,000 or so newly rich Carolina lowcountry elite in a sometimes critical fashion. The energies of the wealthy merchants, planters, and artisans were spent in getting and consuming. This left little time for reading and reflecting. In their scramble for wealth and status most did not live to see 60; for many, old age had set in at 30. But not "given to the great intemperance of the men," a contemporary observed in 1775, the Carolina women usually lived longer.

A few lowcountry citizens were equally critical of the *nouveau riche* as Northern visitors. The eminently regarded Dr. Alexander Garden of Charles Town characterized the new rich as "absolutely above every occupation but eating, drinking, lolling, smoking, and sleeping which five modes constitute the essence of their life and existence." Wealthy gentry steadily tippling rum punch and other cooling drinks on the piazzas of their lowcountry plantations or Charles Town houses during the "dog days" of August contributed to what many contemporaries called the "endemic vice of Carolina," alcoholism.

The Reverend Alexander Hewatt of Charles Town observed in 1775 that "men are distinguished more by their external than internal accomplishments. They are known by the number of their slaves, the value of their annual produce or extent of their landed estate."

To the rich rice and indigo planters, Charles Town, "glittering like the morning-star, full of splendour, vitality, gaiety," was the place to lavishly display and consume their wealth. To contemporaries these "grandiose displays of splendor, debauchery, luxury and extravagance" were the handmaidens of the quick and easy accumulation of riches. Sometimes arrogance too could be measured in direct proportion to their wealth and status. A Philadelphian in Charles Town in the 1770's was jolted when a wealthy resident told him that "Persons coming from the Northward received a polish at Charles Town." Another visitor observed that "the rich [are] haughty and insolent." He attributed this to the ownership of slaves which accustoms the "country gentleman from infancy to tyrannize. They carry with them a disposition to treat all mankind in the same manner." In 1771 when John Rutledge arrogantly denounced the poorer classes of the Carolina hinterlands as a "Pack of Beggars," he was reminded to "look back to your own origins. Step back only to the beginnings of this century. What then was Carolina? What then Charles Town?"

The lowcountry oligarchy of wealthy self-made merchants, planters, and artisans was a new rich class in a rich, new land. This handful of Carolinians constituted an aristocracy based on trade, land, and slaves. They demanded respect for their privileged status. Controlling the economic, social, and political life of the colony, they were quick to defend their positions from assaults from both below and above. And in the early 1760's the assault came from above when the British government switched its laissez-faire policy toward the Colonies to one of close supervision and control. The sharp change in policy galvanized into action a few members of the haughty and proud ruling class. Many others for certain economic, political, and sentimental considerations were slow to act, but eventually act they did.

CHAPTER II

Reluctant Revolutionaries

Hand in hand with the rapacious quest for wealth among the lowcountry's social and political elite went their quest for political power. In South Carolina's Commons House of Assembly, they sought and gained it.

The governmental system in South Carolina as in each of Britain's royal colonies was patterned after the English form. At the head of the government sat the crown-appointed governor representing the interests of the King. Assisting him in his executive and judicial duties was an appointed 12-member Council or Upper House. Rounding out the governmental system was a representative assembly or Lower House. Modeled after the English House of Commons, it was empowered to enact the laws of the colony.

Although English authorities had never intended it to happen, the lowcountry elite by the mid-eighteenth century had made the Assembly the dominant force in the government of the colony. Over the years, the Assembly stripped the Council of its powers on money matters and gained control over the expenditure of public taxes; it came to exercise extensive control over its own membership and proceedings; it arrogated to itself the power to select many of the colony's public officers and even had a hand in shaping the policies of the executive branch.

The popularly elected Assembly offered excellent training in the principles of democratic politics. Here the elite could satisfy their own personal political ambitions while they acted as the guardians of the life, lib-

Courtesy Carolina Art Association/Gibbes Museum of Art
Christopher Gadsden

erty, and property of the people. One royal governor described a member of the South Carolina Assembly as "a zealous stickler for the rights and privileges of the body because he derives his own importance from it." The people, too, came to look on the members of the Assembly as defenders of their liberty and properties.

The Assembly was the only branch of the government whose membership the people could select. At least once every three years nearly every white adult male went to the polls and, using the secret ballot, elected his representatives. Only men with a large "stake in society" stood for election. The minimum requirements were ownership of 500 acres and 10 slaves or the equal in town properties. Such requirements for holding office produced a homogeneous Assembly. Visitors to the Assembly observed that the members "conversed, lolled, and chatted, much like a friendly jovial society." By the 1760's the leadership of the House was in the hands of planters like Thomas Lynch, Rawlins Lowndes, and William Wragg; merchants like Christopher Gadsden and Henry Laurens; and lawyers like John Rutledge, Charles Pinckney, and Peter Manigault. They were public-spirited, unpaid representatives who exchanged their sacrifices of time and energy for the personal rewards of "esteem, admiration, or fame." Schooled in political arts by their tenure in the powerful Assembly, they were quick to meet any challenges to their own personal power and prestige or to the autonomy of the body in local affairs. Their constituents had come to expect no less.

During the early 1760's, the Assembly thwarted a challenge from the royal governor, Thomas Boone. Unsuccessful in his attempt to challenge the Assembly's right to determine the validity of the election of its members, Governor Boone sailed from Charles Town in May, 1764. Perhaps ringing in his ears were the words of his most ardent opponent, Christopher Gadsden—liberty depends upon the possession of "a *free* assembly, *freely* representing a *free* people." However, more conservative members of the Assembly thought Gadsden too hotheaded. Henry Laurens characterized Gadsden in 1764 as a "rash, head-long gentleman who has been too long a ringleader of peoples engaged in popular quarrels." The Assembly gained confidence from their victory over Boone, but soon encountered a more profound challenge.

Faced with a staggering debt incurred in ousting France from North America by 1763 and the need to meet the expense of maintaining a larger permanent standing army there, Great Britain naturally turned to its colonies for revenue. This decision necessitated a radical change in British imperial policy. Strict controls over colonial trade were instituted, and the customs service enforced. Most significantly Parliament passed a series of acts to raise taxes in the Colonies. To some Carolinians one of these measures, the Stamp Act, particularly seemed to threaten their own personal pence and power as well as the autonomy of the Assembly.

Informed that the Stamp Act was pending before Parliament in 1764, the Assembly notified imperial officials of their opposition to its passage. Once again, Christopher Gadsden, known for his relentless pursuit of wealth and power, took the lead in galvanizing the opposition. To Gadsden and other members of the Lower House the measure was inconsistent "with that inherent right of every British subject, not to be taxed but by his own consent, or that of his representative." Despite such opposition from South Carolinians and other colonists, Parliament passed the act in March, 1765. It imposed taxes of varying amounts on such items in the Colonies as legal documents, newspaper advertisements, and playing cards.

To peacefully protest the act, the Massachusetts Assembly called for representatives from each colony to meet in New York in October. The South Carolina House was the first to select delegates to the extra-legal meeting. On August 8, the Assembly chose Gadsden, Thomas

Lynch, a wealthy rice planter, and John Rutledge, who at 26 already possessed an excellent reputation as a Charles Town lawyer. At the Stamp Act Congress they joined with delegates from other Colonies to hammer out a series of resolutions addressed to the King and Parliament "respecting the most Essential Rights and Liberties of the Colonists." Meanwhile, in Charles Town, violent demonstrations were erupting.

During early October, Charles Town citizens read in Peter Timothy's *Gazette* about the extreme actions being taken in other port towns to prevent the sale of stamps. Lawyers, printers, and skilled craftsmen chafed at the idea of buying stamps and the toll it would take on their profits. In public taverns and private homes there were many "hearty damns of the Stamp Act over bottles, bowls and glasses." Local crown officials worried about possible disturbances by "giddy minded" and "evil disposed persons."

Their worst fears were confirmed when the *Planters Adventure* carrying a consignment of stamps sailed into Charles Town harbor on October 18. The following morning a gallows appeared at the intersection of Broad and Church Streets. Inscribed were the words: "Liberty and No Stamp Act." Hanging from the structure was the effigy of a stamp distributor; to its right dangled an effigy of the devil. In the evening the gallows was loaded on a horse-drawn wagon and a mob of several thousand marched beside it as the vehicle rolled eastward down Broad Street. Royal officials were powerless to maintain order. Along the way the mob ransacked the home of George Saxby, the London-appointed stamp collector. The crowd then continued to an open field. Here they burned the effigy and buried a coffin labeled "American Liberty" while the bells of St. Michael's tolled a funeral dirge. Before the mob dispersed, they entered the homes of other suspected stamp officials in search of the hated stamps. Many ended their evening of rifling and searching in local taverns where they drank "Damnation to the Stamp Act." Several nights later a mob disguised in "soot, sailors habits, and slouch hats" roamed through the streets and the homes of prominent officials looking for stamps believed to be secreted in the town. When rumors flew that Henry Laurens was concealing stamps, the mob descended on his home in Ansonborough.

Laurens had received his education in England, formed close friendships there, and his growing fortune was based on trade between mother country and Colonies. At this point the "conservative revolutionary's" loyalty as a British subject took precedence over his belief that the Stamp Act was oppressive. Laurens also deplored mob action. He charactized the Charles Town violence as "burglary and robbery." Although Gadsden was in New York, Laurens believed that this "rash, ringleader of people" was the guiding spirit behind the mob or "Sons of Liberty as they stile themselves." Only when royal Lieutenant Governor William Bull announced that the stamps were not in town and the crown-appointed stamp officials at Charles Town publicly renounced their offices did the nine days of violent demonstrations end.

In late November the Assembly met and approved the resolutions of the Stamp Act Congress. The Lower House also adopted similar resolutions and transmitted them to England. The legislators emphasized that "in taxing ourselves and making laws we can by no means subordinate to any legislative power on earth." In Charles Town a staunch friend of the crown asserted that "the Die is thrown for the Sovereignty of America!" His conclusion was somewhat premature.

With no stamps being issued and no authority to do business without them, the courts closed down and commercial activity dwindled in the Carolina colony. This is precisely what Gadsden and his Sons of Liberty, mainly artisans, desired. Charles Town Liberty Boys believed that by cooperation with their counterparts in Northern ports they could bring trade with England to a halt. This would put economic pressures on English merchants who, in turn, would be compelled to pressure Parliament for repeal of the Stamp Act. Of course, this plan could cut both ways. However, unlike many other factors and merchants, the ambitious Gadsden was willing to suffer immediate financial losses to gain long-range goals; and Gadsden was alert to those merchants who left "nothing untried to poison the minds of the people" to get the ports open. He prowled "the water side at nights to see if anything [was] moving among the shipping."

When the export trade ceased, ships stacked up in the harbor. Barrels of rice cluttered the wharves and idle seamen thronged the taverns of the town. The profits of merchants and planters plummeted. Pressures on Gadsden and his Liberty Boys eventually forced them to back down. Also demands by the wealthy elite in the Assembly forced Lieutenant Governor William Bull to permit ships to clear the port under certain conditions by early 1766.

Charles Town lawyers, as "cautious revolutionaries" as the merchants and planters, also wanted to resist and make money at the same time. They sought to open the courts for business, but without the required stamps.

Forced to compromise, Gadsden continued to oppose the act in principle. His principles drew only sneers from many of the elite. Henry Laurens observed bemusedly in late January that Gadsden and his Liberty

Boys are "pretty quiet" now. The reluctant rebel Laurens contemptuously observed that some of the Sons of Liberty are repenting in "having interfered in matters which did not come properly under their cognisance."

The opposition in the Colonies and in England prompted Parliament to repeal the Stamp Act in March. But to pacify opponents of repeal within their own body, Parliament passed the Declaratory Act at the same time. It stated that the American Colonies were subordinate to Parliament, which possessed the power to legislate for the Colonies "in all cases whatsoever." But Americans overlooked the ominous wording of the act in their rush to embrace the news of the repeal of the Stamp Act. Most thought that the British government had acquiesced to their views.

In early May one of the vessels bringing news of the repeal of the Stamp Act to Charles Town broke up near the bar at the harbor's mouth in "very thick weather" and an easterly gale. The survivors eventually spread the news.

Speaker of the Assembly, Peter Manigault, recalled: "All was Joy, Jollity and Mirth"; Christopher Gadsden "was so overcome at hearing the news that he almost fainted." Spontaneous celebrations broke out across the town. Militia companies paraded through the streets, and at night the windows of the town sparkled with candles put there to celebrate the repeal. After the official word reached the Carolina colony, a celebration seldom seen in Charles Town got underway on June 4. It coincided with King George III's birthday. Church bells rang, ships in the harbor unfurled their colors, cannons boomed, and standing side by side, royal officials and members of the Assembly watched militia companies pass in review down Broad Street. Two days later, the Assembly prepared an address to the King

Courtesy Carolina Art Association/Gibbes Museum of Art

Peter Manigault, Speaker of the South Carolina Assembly, 1760's,
Dining with Some Friends

thanking him for his "great goodness" by bringing
about the repeal of the Stamp Act. In forwarding the
resolutions to England, Speaker of the House Manigault
wrote that these documents show "the inhabitants of
this province [to be] a loyal and a grateful people." The
House also voted funds to erect a marble statue to the
advocate of their cause in Parliament, William Pitt, who
gave "noble and generous assistance towards obtaining
the repeal of the Stamp Act." When the statue was put in
place on July 5, 1770, at the intersection of Broad and
Meeting Streets, it was the first of a public man in
America. The toga-wrapped figure depicted the statesman with upraised arm, obviously extended to em-
phasize the rights of the colonists. During the siege of
Charles Town in 1780, a British shell severed the limb.
The statue stands today in Washington Park behind City
Hall.

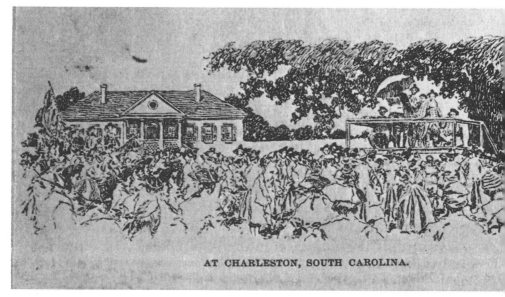

AT CHARLESTON, SOUTH CAROLINA.

Courtesy South Carolina Historical Society

A Public Meeting at the Liberty Tree

Only a few Americans recognized that by the wording of the Declaratory Act, Parliament was pointing out the subordinate status of the Colonies. Among the few Americans to realize this was Christopher Gadsden. Like several New England and Virginia zealots, Gadsden saw in the wording of the act ominous signs for the future of American liberties. In the fall of 1766, he summoned Charles Town's Sons of Liberty to meetings under a beautiful live oak just outside the town's limits. To the "Liberty Tree" came mainly the artisans of the town — well-to-do and influential men like William Johnson, a blacksmith; the painter George Flagg; Daniel Cannon, carpenter; and Edward Weyman, the upholsterer. Here it was reported that Gadsden "harangued" them "on the folly of relaxing their opposition and vigilance" in the face of Great Britain's "designs or pretensions." At this time in sharp disagreement with men of his own class, Gadsden was nearly alone among the Charles Town elite promoting the "natural and inherent rights" of Englishmen in America. Already Gadsden was talking about his willingness to sacrifice his life at "the altar of liberty and in the cause of my country." Soon again, however, actions by the crown threatened the pence and power of the lowcountry elite. Royal officialdom played into the hands of zealots like Gadsden. They helped him rally more "cautious revolutionaries" to the cause.

In the spring of 1767, a new royal customs collector, Daniel Moore, arrived in Charles Town. It soon became apparent that Moore was as interested in tightening up the customs service as in increasing his own personal fortunes. He began vigorously enforcing trade regulations which benefited him financially. Merchants, angered by his vigor and tactics, brought complaints and suits in the courts.

John Neufville and Gabriel Manigault instituted suit against Moore for requiring "fees, gratuities or rewards for signing several Indigo Certificates." When the coastal schooners *Broughton Island Packet* and *Wambaw* owned by Henry Laurens did not clear port according to the exact letter of the law, Moore seized the vessels. Laurens not only brought suit against the customs collector, but was so infuriated that he accosted Moore on a crowded Charles Town street and twisted his nose.

Shortly after this encounter and with suits against him still pending, Moore fled to England. Now Laurens pushed his case in the courts against the royal customs searcher George Roupell who physically had seized the vessels. A new royal customs collector, Roger P. H. Hatley, then conspired with Roupell and authorized the seizure of the *Ann*, a vessel partly owned by Laurens. When Roupell offered to release the ship if Laurens dropped his charges, Laurens refused.

The case dragged on into 1768 before the juryless Vice-Admiralty Court of the crown-appointed Judge Egerton Leigh. Although Leigh ordered the release of Laurens' schooners, he disallowed the claim against Roupell for damages. Laurens was outraged. Customs officials had harassed him and tried extortion; the case had been time-consuming; his ships had been tied up and lawyer fees and court costs had been expensive. His pence, power, and reputation had been assailed. Moreover, Laurens thought that justice had been sacrificed to Judge Leigh's own self-interest and protection of the crown's customs officials. He came to believe that the arbitrary powers of men like Leigh were potentially dangerous to his own interest and those of other Americans. "Such officers are the most likely instruments to effect a disunion between the Mother Country and her American offspring," Laurens wrote. Through widely-circulated pamphlets he launched attacks on Leigh, the juryless Vice-Admiralty Court, and racketeering customs officials.

His pamphlets found a wide audience throughout the Colonies, particularly in Boston where John Hancock was locked in quarrels similar to Laurens'. The "cautious revolutionary" Henry Laurens was becoming a strident advocate of American rights. Other lowcountry factors, merchants, and planters were moving more slowly down the path first cut by Gadsden and his Liberty Boys. But already events abroad were underway which would push the reluctant rebels further along the path toward resistance.

Still faced with the need to raise revenue from the Colonies following repeal of the Stamp Act, Parliament passed the Townshend Acts in 1767. These measures imposed taxes on all glass, lead, paint, paper, and tea imported into America. First in Boston, the cockpit of dissent, then in towns of the Middle Colonies the famil-

iar cry went up: "no taxation without representation."
By late 1768, a crown official in Charles Town was
writing his superiors in England warning that there
were "many here who entertain the political principles
now prevailing in Boston." When the South Carolina
Assembly endorsed a circular letter sent by the Massachusetts Assembly urging resistance to the
Townshend Acts by boycotting British products, the
House met the same fate as the one in Massachusetts —
their respective royal governors dissolved the assemblies. These actions played into the hands of Christopher Gadsden who jumped at the chance to resist
royal officialdom by extra-legal methods. He called out
his Liberty Boys, and they were soon parading, ha-
ranguing, and organizing for a boycott of British goods.

The prompt rallying of the artisans to Gadsden's sum-
mons was partly due to the Townshend duties so sharply slicing into their profits. They now experienced the
economic threat which the elite merchants, planters,
and lawyers had experienced following passage of the
Stamp Act. Taxes on imported glass bore heavily on
builders like Daniel Cannon; Townshend's taxes on imported printers' colors and white lead fell with equal
weight on artists like George Flagg. Already pinched
financially by a shortage of coin in the colony, the requirements to pay the Townshend taxes in specie also
angered the artisans; and since the Townshend Acts
permitted crown officers to search without warrants in
places suspected of harboring untaxed goods, the artisans viewed this feature of the act as a further invasion
of their rights as Englishmen.

Planters, too, chafed at the threats to their civil and
economic liberties under the new act. Scarcity of money
already had limited their ability to pay off debts to
merchants at home and abroad. Additional syphoning
off of gold and silver could be financially disastrous.

The merchants, however, were not as directly affected by the Townshend Acts. If they imported and paid duties on glass, lead, paper, and tea, the merchants could raise the prices of these items to their customers. Therefore, when the planters began to travel along the same path as Gadsden and the artisans who advocated boycotts, the merchants initially refused to budge. Their pence was not pinched by the Townshend Acts; a boycott of British goods, however, could mean financial ruin for them.

Speaking for many merchants, displaying his own interests, personal loyalties to the crown, and fears of the financial effects of a boycott, William Henry Drayton publicly blasted the organizer of the resistance, Christopher Gadsden. The young, wealthy Drayton, recently returned to Charles Town from Oxford, attacked Gadsden as a "vain demagogue." Drayton condemned "the patriotism of the age" which denied a person the liberty of "thinking and reasoning." No true patriot and friend of liberty would resist the fundamental laws of his country, he declared. To him, Gadsden was therefore a lunatic who should be incarcerated in the madhouse at public expense.

Despite such opposition, artisans and planters "at public meetings in taverns or under the Liberty Tree" continued to support a boycott during the summer of 1769. Outnumbered, fearing more extreme actions, the merchants eventually moved for a compromise. After a series of small private and public meetings where representatives from the artisan's, planter's, and merchant's communities hammered out arguments on which items would be subject to boycott, a large public gathering was called on July 22. With Christopher Gadsden presiding, a compromise was agreed to by the three interest groups. Most British manufactured products were prohibited; however, merchants could import for sale such items as tools, firearms, hardware, cheap cloth, and printed books. Further importation of slaves was not allowed since it drained lowcountry specie, and slave labor often competed with the artisans.

On the same day, a committee of 13 artisans, 13 planters, and 13 merchants was selected to gather signatures to the agreements and take any "necessary steps" in seeing that the boycott was *most strictly* adhered to." The committee adopted the intimidating, perhaps double-meaning, motto: "Sign or Die." Showing that they meant business, the committee occasionally threatened to use violence and social and political ostracism against those who hesitated to sign. It is small wonder that by early August 142 persons had signed.

There were those who refused to cooperate. These non-signers either placed loyalty to British law or their own personal financial interests or both above support of an extra-legal boycott. A prominent importer, the merchant John Gordon, refused under pressure "to be bandied about" by the committee. Staunch crown supporter William Wragg, who condemned the illegality of the committee, asserted that he refused to be "directed by capricious men not having authority." William Henry Drayton also refused to sign. He put loyalty to Parliamentary law above what he believed an unlawful combination of designing men. Resentful of the emergence of the artisans in politics and their leadership of the non-importation movement, Drayton contemptuously blasted them for not knowing their place. He labeled them the "profanus vulgus."

In the early fall of 1769 at a gathering under the Liberty Tree, Gadsden publicly stigmatized Drayton and some 30 others who had refused to sign the non-importation agreement. Shortly afterwards, Drayton sailed for England where he hoped his views would find a more ready audience. Back in Charles Town in 1772, events would transform young Drayton's attitudes toward British policy.

Since other port towns also adopted boycotts, trade with England dropped off sharply in 1769. The non-importation agreement proved particularly effective at Charles Town. Within a year imports declined over 50 percent. In December, 1769, usually a bustling, busy month about the wharves, few sails could be seen in the harbor.

While Charles Town merchants unhappily bore the burden of the declining trade, artisans celebrated. Profits soared for some when they turned to manufacturing and offered goods for sale labeled "made in Carolina." Taking advantage of the political climate, one shrewd artisan enjoyed a lively trade in homemade "liberty umbrellas." Some lowcountry residents made their own clothing. In late August the *South Carolina Gazette* praised this practice, noting that a gentleman living near Charles Town had spun, woven, knitted, or tanned his own outfit—"His shirt was of fine linen, his coat of fustian, his jacket of dimity, his breeches buckskin, his stockings thread," and his shoes of leather.

Once again the colonial boycott of British goods accomplished the desired result. With their trade and profits declining sharply, English merchants petitioned Parliament to repeal the Townshend Acts. In April, 1770, Parliament acted. All duties under the Townshend Acts were repealed except the tax on tea. Now, one by one, New York, Virginia, Maryland, and North Carolina abandoned their non-importation schemes. Some lowcountry leaders, however, agonized over the rush to resume trade. They realized that the real cause of colonial grievances remained. By retaining the tax on tea, Parliament had asserted its right to levy any additional taxes in the future. The personal pence and power of the ambitious lowcountry elite, their rights and those of fellow colonists, and the autonomy of Carolina's Lower House of Assembly were still threatened by Parliamentary power.

Despite scattered pleas for continuing the boycott, the momentum grew for ending non-importation at Charles Town in view of the general collapse of colonial resistance and the pressures of local merchants. On December 13, 1770, a general meeting of the citizens of the town convened to consider ending the boycott. Henry Laurens, eschewing his earlier stance on the Stamp Act, now warmly embracing non-importation, was elected presiding officer. As the meeting got underway, an observer noted that Thomas Lynch and John Mackenzie, planters, and Christopher Gadsden in defending continuation of the boycott "exerted eloquence and rhetorical tears for the expiring liberties" of America. But their "struggle tho' strong proved ineffectual." The "general voice was yea" to end non-importation.

The Carolinians were the last among the colonists to lift the boycott. During the struggle against the Townshend Acts more and more men of property had joined Gadsden and his Liberty Boys at the cutting edge of radical resistance to imperial authority. Nor did one royal official at Charles Town see any end to the agitation. He believed there were about the town too many radical "busy spirits." His assumptions were correct.

With the revival of trade following repeal of the Townshend Acts, prosperity returned, and Anglo-American tensions ebbed in nearly every colony except Massachusetts and South Carolina. In the Southern colony, events were already in the saddle. They would play into the hands of Charles Town's "busy spirits" who would ride them forward toward revolution. One of these events was the Wilkes Fund Dispute.

The origins of the dispute began in London. During the 1760's a demagogic member of Parliament, John Wilkes, in edition No. 45 of his *North Briton* newspaper criticized a speech by George III. Wilkes was promptly thrown into prison and expelled from Parliament. After release from prison he continued to boldly oppose the King and in 1768 was re-elected to Parliament. Wilkes was not allowed to take his seat, and charges were again renewed against him for seditious libel of the King; he was returned to prison. To men in America Wilkes' struggle against crown and Parliament seemed to symbolize their own struggles against an "oppressive" government which had imposed unconstitutional taxes on them.

By the end of the 1760's, the *South Carolina Gazette*, edited by Peter Timothy, one of Gadsden's Liberty Boys, was referring to Wilkes as the "unshaken colossus of freedom"; Gadsden himself, enlisted by Wilkes' friends in England who sought political and financial support for the imprisoned reformer, introduced into South Carolina's Commons House of Assembly their request for funds. In early December, 1769, the Assembly voted to send 1,500 pounds sterling to Wilkes' friends in England.

The contribution of the House to Wilkes, the only act of its kind in the Colonies, was an insult to imperial authorities and to the King who viewed Wilkes as a common criminal. Even more outrageous to the English government was the fact that the money had been appropriated without the required approval of the royal governor and his council which would have doubtlessly vetoed it. Angry imperial authorities responded to the Assembly's act in April, 1770. South

Carolina's royal governor was instructed to strip the Assembly of its rights to initiate action on money matters and to bar any effort by the Assembly in future tax bills to raise money for the South Carolina Treasury to replace the funds voted to Wilkes. By this latter measure, imperial authorities sought to force the Assembly into repudiating the funds.

To the elite of South Carolina's Commons House, Thomas Lynch, Rawlins Lowndes, Henry Laurens, Christopher Gadsden, John Mackenzie, and Charles Cotesworth Pinckney, this imperial fiat threatened the hard-won prerogatives on money matters gained by the Assembly over the years and its very autonomy in local affairs. Laurens spoke for these powerful social and political leaders when he declared that at stake was "nothing less than the very Essence of pure liberty." It was the sole "Right of the people" through their elective representatives to decide questions touching the raising and spending of taxes. The issue was joined. Royal governor and Assembly would soon clash.

During the summer of 1770, support for the cause of John Wilkes moved from the Assembly into the streets. By the time that the citizens of Charles Town raised on July 5, 1770, the statue to their Parliamentary champion on the Stamp Act issue, William Pitt, their old hero had been eclipsed by the new, John Wilkes. On that day members of Charles Town's Club No. 45, their sobriquet being chosen in honor of the 45th edition of Wilkes' *North Briton,* paraded through the streets shouting "huzzas" to Pitt, Wilkes, and liberty. To cap the day of celebrating, they assembled at Dillon's and drank 45 toasts. While they drank to King, Royal Family, and Parliament, the members of Club No. 45 also drank to the Sons of Liberty, "the men who will part with Life before Liberty," to Gadsden, Lynch, and John Rutledge.

But the last toast was raised to John Wilkes, "may [he] always prove a scourge to tyrants."

With the autumn of 1771 came the inevitable clash between the Assembly and royal Governor Charles Montagu. When the Commons House requested the colony's two treasurers to disburse money from the treasury and they refused without the agreement of governor and council, the Assembly ordered them jailed for contempt of its authority. To prevent incarceration of the treasurers, Montagu dissolved the Assembly on November 5. Convening again in April 1772, the House refused to transact any business until permitted solely to draft and pass a tax bill. Once again, Montagu impatiently dissolved the Assembly. Determined to bend the Commons House to the imperial will, Montagu next hit upon a plan to harass and inconvenience his opposition in the Assembly. By this he hoped to prod the body into transacting business as usual. Putting his plan into operation, he called a meeting of the Assembly at Beaufort, a coastal town some 70 miles to the south. Roaring its disapproval and reflecting the attitude of the leading members of the Assembly, a Charles Town newspaper declared: "No measure of any Governor was more freely and generally condemned."

Montagu's ploy failed. When the House members reconvened in Charles Town in the fall of 1772, they passed a series of resolutions charging the governor with "an unwarrantable abuse of a Royal prerogative" and called for his removal. Proroguing the Assembly twice more to protect himself, Montagu was nevertheless unable to command respect or obedience from a House membership united in its will to protect its rights from the threat of imperial intimidation. By 1773, Montagu had returned to England and resigned in disgrace.

With Montagu's departure the 12-member Governor's Council now attempted to prod the Commons into carrying out its normal legislative functions. For several years, all legislation had been at a standstill, and no tax bill had been passed by the House due to the Wilkes Fund Dispute. The president of the Council, Sir Egerton Leigh, attempted to take matters into his own hands. Unfortunately for the crown's interests, however, Leigh was already a social pariah among Charles Town's economic and political elite. As judge of the Vice-Admiralty Court, Leigh had infuriated Henry Laurens and others by his self-seeking and capricious actions. Furthermore, it was common knowledge that Leigh had seduced and made pregnant his own ward who was his wife's sister and Lauren's niece. Indirectly, Leigh had caused the death of the child produced by the union. Laurens believed that in consideration of Leigh's background, "He is the most wicked man and the greatest fool that ever I heard or read of." One Charles Town resident believed that citizens looked on Leigh as the greatest "rascal among all the King's friends. He has great merit in this reign."

To prod the Assembly into passing a tax bill to raise money necessary to support the normal functions of government, Leigh had the Council prepare a report blaming the House for the exhausted provincial treasury. When two members of the Council dissented and drafted a manifesto condemning the Council's actions and leaked it to the *South Carolina Gazette*, Leigh was furious. He ordered the arrest of the printer, Thomas Powell, for violating the privileges of the Council. Members of the Assembly immediately denounced the arrest as an illegal act since the Council was merely an advisory body and lacked the authority to commit a person for contempt. Powell was soon released, Leigh publicly denounced, and eventually he, too, departed

Carolina unwept, unsung, and, perhaps regrettably to some, unhung.

By late 1773, members of the Carolina Assembly had weathered threats to their rights and prerogatives. Still no tax bill had passed the House. It had stood down a demanding governor, forced him to depart in disgrace, contributed to the eclipse of the power of the Council, and prompted its "scandalous" royal appointee, Leigh, to depart in defeat. Eventually, after four years of legislative inaction, with the colony in its fifth year without a tax bill, the Assembly asserted its own will. Without the approval of royal officials, it issued certificates of indebtedness to pay off long-standing public debts.

The Wilkes Fund Dispute revealed that South Carolina's leaders were determined that royal authorities respect their long-standing local practices and precedents. When crown officials did not, the Assembly was now willing to proceed without their approval. A giant step had been taken down the road toward Revolution.

The legality of the Assembly's actions revolving around the Wilkes Fund Dispute would be challenged by imperial officials up to the very eve of the revolt. But by 1773 the clouds of other events even more threatening to the personal wealth and power of the lowcountry elite and their Assembly were gathering on the horizon. One of these was the move by Parliament to serve powerful financial interests in England by giving the East India Company a virtual monopoly on tea trade to America.

Subject to a duty of only three pence per pound, the East India Company's tea consigned directly to a few favored importers permitted them to sell the product to consumers at a lower price than most American merchants could and still realize a profit. This plan neatly coin-with the crown's interests. By taxing the tea imported into America, the British government could assert its authority so rudely challenged by the colonists — the right of Parliament to tax the colonists. But once again, the Americans viewed the duty on imported tea, like the duties under the Stamp and Townshend Acts, as a tax designed to raise revenue and one levied without their consent. Acceptance of the dutied tea would be an admission that the power of taxation reposed in the body where Americans were not represented. Their personal pence and the power of their Assembly were again threatened.

In the autumn of 1773, seven ships dropped down the Thames and into the open sea. Stowed in their holds were 2,000 chests of East India Company tea consigned to merchants in Boston, New York, Philadelphia, and Charles Town. Captain Alexander Curling, universally respected as a "gentleman" and admired for "his skill and seamanship," steered the *London* for the Southern port. It carried 257 chests consigned to agents of the East India Company. Seven weeks later, Captain Curling's ship appeared off Charles Town. On the evening tide of Wednesday, December 1, he ran the *London* over the bar and came to anchor in the harbor.

For weeks rumors had been rife that a cargo of tea was destined for Charles Town. Timothy, through his *Gazette*, and Gadsden, among his Liberty Boys, had encouraged local resistance to the landing of the tea and the collection of duties. Now with the rumors confirmed, these radicals and their followers sped the word to Dillon's and Ramage's Taverns and throughout the town on the morning of December 2. Acceptance of the tea would "establish a *precedent;* confirm the *power assumed* by Parliament to pass laws BINDING AMONG THE COLONIES in all cases whatsoever," they argued. Such a precedent would render their local Assembly impotent. By mid-day Thursday, handbills were circulating across the town, and notices were posted along Broad Street inviting "all the inhabitants, particularly the landholders, to assemble in the Great Hall over the Exchange at 3 o'clock on Friday afternoon." The "sense of the people" would be taken and plans formulated on what should be done about the recently arrived cargo of tea.

Since the Assembly had ceased to function because of the Wilkes Fund Dispute, options for an organized protest to landing the tea had been narrowed. The meeting called at the Exchange Building by such radical leaders as Gadsden and Timothy offered the more "conservative revolutionaries" an opportunity for an organized protest.

Mainly artisans and planters crowded into the Great Hall of the Exchange at the foot of Broad Street by 3 o'clock Friday afternoon, December 3. Believing that they had the most to lose, these two groups had led the resistance to earlier Parliamentary revenue schemes. For the opposite reasons and as they had done before, the merchant-importers hung back. Only a few attended the meeting.

The meeting got underway when "a very worthy and honorable gentleman," Colonel George Gabriel Powell, was unanimously elected to preside. A zealous advocate of American rights in the Assembly, owner of extensive tracts along the Pee Dee some distance from Charles Town, a colonel in the Craven County militia, Powell was considered somewhat of an outsider in the lowcountry clash of interests between artisans, planters, and merchants. It was thought perhaps that such a man could best unite the local discordant groups.

After some debate, a document was drafted to read: "We the undersigned, do hereby agree, not to import, either directly or indirectly, any teas that will pay the present duty laid by an act of the British Parliament for the purpose of raising a revenue in America." A committee was then appointed to circulate the resolution and secure the signatures of all merchants engaged in the import trade. Several of the merchants present stepped forward to sign the agreement, but others "were cool, and differed in the reasonableness and utility" of the resolution.

Before the conclusion of the meeting, agents of the East India Company and consignees of the cargo of tea, Roger Smith, Peter Leger, and William Greenwood, were summoned. When the three merchants appeared, members of the assemblage quickly convinced them by "threats and flatterys" that they should not receive the tea. Greeting the merchants' decision with clapping and roars of approval, the crowd shortly flowed out of the Great Hall and into the fading light of the late December afternoon.

It had been a day fraught with great significance. "Cautious revolutionaries" had moved from their legally constituted Lower House of Assembly because it had ceased to function and joined with the radical activists of the streets to meet indoors at an extra-legal, but orderly, gathering governed by parliamentary rules. Missing, however, had been most of the ultraconservative mercantile community. It was now up to the artisans and planters to secure the merchants' approval and support.

The five-member committee appointed to obtain signatures of the merchants represented the merger of "cautious revolutionaries" and street activists. Charles Pinckney, his first cousin Charles Cotesworth Pinckney, and Thomas Ferguson were well-to-do lowcountry planters and all long-time members of the Lower House of Assembly. Rounding out the committee were two equally powerful and wealthy men, Christopher Gadsden and Daniel Cannon. Although Gadsden had been a leading firebrand in the Lower House, he was better known for his harangues under the Liberty Tree. Cannon had never sat in the Assembly, but the wealthy building contractor and property owner who gave his name to Cannonsboro had long since joined Gadsden in his out-of-doors activities.

Despite the pressures of this committee of wealthy and powerful men to enlist the merchants, a group of equally influential members of the mercantile community refused to cooperate. It was a matter of profits and losses. Many merchants already had tea on hand or had placed orders for it. To counter the pressures on them to agree to the December 3 resolution, they met in Mrs. Swallow's Tavern on Broad Street on December 9. Here they organized the Charles Town Chamber of Commerce. John Savage was elected the first president. He had accumulated a fortune in trade as a partner of Gabriel Manigault. Miles Brewton, Charles Town's greatest importer of slaves and one of the lowcountry's wealthiest citizens, became vice president. These men were represented at another general meeting at the Exchange on December 17. Despite protests from the mercantile community, a resolution was endorsed which prohibited the landing or vending of tea until the tea tax was repealed.

Perhaps angered at the opposition to the boycott by the profit-minded merchants, more radical spirits anonymously threatened to burn the tea ship London. But there was no disorder. Because no one appeared to receive and pay the duty on the tea aboard the London within 21 days after its arrival, crown officials seized the tea on December 22. That was the law. It was landed and stored in the cellar of the Exchange.

Perhaps the lack of unified resistance in Charles Town prevented the type of reaction which occurred elsewhere. During December in Boston, tea was dumped and destroyed; citizens in New York and Philadelphia turned the tea ships back. Even though the crown thought that the Charles Town tea party was "not equal in criminality to the proceedings in other Colonies," George III considered it "a most unwarrantable insult to the authority of the Kingdom."

Charles Town firebrands were plunged into remorse, not at the anger of the crown, but that they had not acted with the vigor of their radical allies to the north. Peter Timothy thought it to Charles Town's shame that it was the only port in America where tea had been landed.

To compensate for their failure to unify opposition to prevent the landing of the tea, Charles Town's Liberty Boys stepped up their campaign for resistance. Calling a general meeting of the citizens on March 16, members of the Sons of Liberty met the evening before at "the Lodge-Room in Lodge Alley" to rededicate themselves to resistance. Here they resolved that "their present conduct depends whether they shall in the future be taxed by any other than representatives of their choice — and whether this hitherto respectable province shall preserve its reputation, or sink into Disgrace and Contempt." The next day at the general meeting, Liberty Boys led the movement to establish a "Standing General Committee." Its function was to act as a temporary executive branch and to rally the people against any further efforts at tea importation.

A few months later the captains of several tea ships which appeared in Charles Town's harbor were threatened with physical violence. In early November, 1774, when it was discovered that the recently arrived *Britannia* carried seven chests of tea consigned to merchants in Charles Town, the General Committee forced the consignees to board the ship, smash in the chests, and empty the contents into the Cooper River. A few days later, several thousand citizens paraded through the streets to the city limits. Here they cheered the burning of effigies of "abbetors of American taxation," agents of the King, and a large quantity of tea donated by the householders of Charles Town. The tide was turning in the radicals' direction. Rushing it to flood stage were events in England.

Shocked and angered by the tea parties in America, particularly the one in Boston, the English government resolved "to pursue such measures as shall be effectual for securing the Dependence of the colonies upon the Kingdom." The first of these measures passed Parliament in early 1774. It closed the port of Boston to commerce. Shortly afterwards a second act provided for the trial in England of any royal official committing a capital offense in America; and a third measure sharply altered the governmental system of Massachusetts. Called the Coercive Acts in England, they were labeled the Intolerable Acts by colonists.

Intended to intimidate all Americans, though aimed primarily at Boston, the acts elicited the opposite response from radical and "cautious revolutionary" alike at Charles Town. Local firebrand and editor Peter Timothy brought out an extra edition of the *Gazette* with bold black borders containing the entire wording of the acts. Henry Laurens denounced the Coercive Acts as precedents for laws to "cram down every mandate which ministers shall think proper for keeping us in subjection to the Task Master who shall be put over us."

The Coercive measures even outraged and roused William Henry Drayton, so long "attached to the king's person and government," to publicly denounce "the malignant nature of the Acts." It may have been more than outrage at the Coercive Acts which prompted Drayton to drastically alter his sympathies. He had been bumped from a lucrative office by a crown official. Another royal appointee had thwarted his scheme for land speculation, and he was heavily in debt to British creditors. Whatever the reason for his sudden shift of loyalties, Henry Laurens referred to Drayton in 1774 as "our converted countryman." Like a convert to religion, Drayton's zeal for the cause outdid older advocates.

Seeing their own fate linked with that of the Northerners, citizens of the lowcountry, determined to aid the beleaguered Bostonians during the summer of 1774, with other South Carolinians, sent more rice and cash to the Northern port town than any other colony. The General Committee at Charles Town also issued a call throughout the colony for a General Meeting at the Exchange Building in early July. Charles Town's leading radical, Christopher Gadsden, wrote his counterpart in Boston, Sam Adams, that he had hopes "that this affair relating to your government will effectually rouse" the people of the Carolinas. Gadsden was not disappointed.

The General Meeting began in Charles Town on July 6. For the first time an extra-legal body in the port town had drawn representatives from nearly every county and parish across the colony. Edward Rutledge observed that "almost every man of consequence" attended. The meeting lasted three days. Resolutions condemning the Coercive Acts were quickly adopted. The next order of business took a bit longer—the selection of delegates to a general congress proposed by the Assembly of Massachusetts to meet in Philadelphia in September.

Wranglings began when the ultraconservative larger merchants suggested one slate of delegates and the more radical-minded artisans and planters offered another. A compromise of sorts was worked out, however, when the instructions to the delegates were worded to satisfy all factions; and when Henry Middle-

William Henry Drayton

Charles Pinckney

ton and John Rutledge, nominated by every interest group, were elected along with Christopher Gadsden, Thomas Lynch, and Edward Rutledge. The new-found harmony among the factions was further sealed by the election of Colonel Charles Pinckney as Chairman of the Committee of 99. Composed of 15 merchants, 15 artisans, and 69 planters, among the Committee's responsibilities was the handling of executive matters for fu-

John Rutledge

ture general meetings. For all intents and purposes it
became the temporary government of South Carolina.

Despite some appearance of unanimity in Charles Town
by the late summer of 1774, there still existed sharp
differences of opinion on crown-colony relationships.
Among the clergy, it was manifest. While the Presbyterian Reverend William Tennent of the Independent
Church cast his bread into the radical current through
printed sermons and anonymous letters to the press, the

Courtesy Independence National Historical Park Collection, Philadelphia
Edward Rutledge

Anglican Reverend John Bullman, assistant minister at St. Michael's, stood by the established government and preached pro-crown sentiments from his pulpit.

To the Reverend Tennent the dispute between England and America had reached the point as to whether or not the Colonies "shall be reduced to a State of the most abject slavery." Through the Charles Town *Gazette* and

Country Journal of August 2, 1774, Tennent appealed to the ladies "to lend their hands to save America from the dagger of tyranny." Just under two weeks later, the Reverend Bullman preached against "every silly clown" who censures a monarch or government. Such actions, he said, lead only to "sedition and rebellion." But the prevailing winds of sentiment were blowing Tennent's way. A majority of the vestry and parishioners of St. Michael's voted to oust Bullman for his remarks.

In late August, South Carolina's five delegates to the First Continental Congress departed Charles Town by ship bound for Philadelphia. They were similar in many ways. All were born in Charles Town or nearby and were wealthy and socially prominent. Henry Middleton owned nearly 50,000 acres of land and 800 slaves; Gadsden was an eminently successful factor and land speculator; Thomas Lynch owned rich rice lands along the Santee; the Rutledge brothers were English-trained lawyers with flourishing law practices in Charles Town. All criticized British policy after 1763 and with the exception of Edward Rutledge were members of the South Carolina Assembly. Only Gadsden spoke for the radicals; the others supported the more conservative planter class. They did vary considerably in age. Middleton was the oldest at 57, Edward Rutledge the youngest at 25.

Meeting in Philadelphia at Carpenters Hall from September 5 to October 26, 1774, the First Continental Congress as an extra-legal body enacted measures which moved Americans closer to revolution. A majority of the delegates voted to condemn the Coercive Acts, adopted a "Continental Association" pledging Americans to boycott most British goods, sent a formal list of grievances to the English government, and resolved to meet again if redress was not forthcoming by May, 1775.

Philosophically more in tune with the radical domi-
nated Congress, Gadsden and Lynch played a more con-
spicuous role and were more warmly characterized by
fellow delegates than the conservative Middleton and
the Rutledges. Gadsden at 50 years of age was as impul-
sive and zealous as ever. A Connecticut delegate described him as leaving "all New England Sons of Liberty
far behind, for he is for taking up his firelock and marching direct to Boston." Lynch impressed fellow members
as a "solid" man who "carries with him more force in
his very appearance than most powdered folks in their
conversation." John Adams did not trust the conservative John Rutledge. Adams found him to be a man with
an "air of reserve, design, and cunning." The Virginia
firebrand, Patrick Henry, feared that the Rutledges
along with other conservative delegates might "ruin the
cause of America."

One of the most dramatic incidents at the First Continental Congress came when four of the South Carolina
delegates walked out of the meeting in protest of the
Continental Association. Only the firebrand Gadsden,
true to his nature, refused to join the protest. Led by John
Rutledge and thinking in terms of profits and losses,
they refused to sign the non-importation, non-con-
sumption, and non-exportation embargo against England which included indigo and rice. Prohibiting the
export of the lowcountry's two main crops, Rutledge
believed, would financially ruin the planter class. Seeking colonial unity, the delegates at the Congress were
willing to compromise. Planters were permitted to export rice, but the prohibition on indigo exportation remained. On October 20 the four delegates walked back
into the Congress and with Gadsden signed the Association. Many lowcountry merchants and planters still desired profits with their protests.

Shortly after the five South Carolinians returned from Philadelphia to Charles Town, the General Committee of 99 called for colony-wide elections of representatives to a General Meeting. Many of the elected representatives to the General Meeting which convened at Charles Town in the Long Room of Pike's Tavern on January 11, 1775, were also members of the Assembly. With the legal government of the colony nearly moribund, the General Meeting quickly transformed itself into the First Provincial Congress. This direct descendent of the December 3, 1773, meeting at the Exchange assumed the legislative power for the colony. It included the socially and politically elite planters and merchants — as well as the prominent radical artisans, Peter Timothy, Daniel Cannon, Joshua Lockwood, and Edward Weyman. Symbolic of their new-found power and organization, the representatives moved their meeting to the Assembly's wing of the State House. Here Henry Laurens reported that the 180-odd delegates sat "with all the solemnity and formality of a constitutional parliament." South Carolina's Provincial Congress endorsed the actions of the First Continental Congress and South Carolina's delegates by electing them to return to the Second. It created committees of safety and observation to enforce the non-importation, non-exportation agreements of the Association. Before adjourning in mid-January, the Provincial Congress issued the ominous warning that South Carolinians should "be diligently attentive in learning the use of arms."

The first attempts to break the embargo quickly moved Charles Town's Committee of Observation to action. In late February the *Charming Sally* out of Bristol appeared in the harbor carrying salt, tiles, and coal consigned to local merchants. The Committee prevented off-loading of the merchandise, and the consignees, unable to afford reshipment, suffered heavy financial losses when they had to dump the goods into Hog Island Creek.

Extreme and vigilant support for the embargo ran particularly strong among the artisans and laborers. In March a resident of the town returning aboard ship from England requested the landing of furniture and horses for his own personal use. Under these circumstances, the Committee of Safety first decided to allow him to bring the goods ashore. However, when a mob led by Gadsden appeared at dockside and threatened to shoot the horses if they were landed, the Committee reversed itself. A royal official observing the incident worried over the "many headed power of the People, who have discovered their own strength and importance." He believed that never again will they be "so easily governed by their former leaders." Given this climate of opinion in Charles Town and throughout the Colonies, when the news arrived of Parliament's acts in response to the First Continental Congress, it was interpreted as meaning further coercion, not conciliation. To many it meant war. Both radicals and royal officials looked to their powder and arms.

In Massachusetts "minute men" at Lexington and Concord unsuccessfully attempted to defend their hoard of weapons from seizure on April 19 and fired "the shots heard round the world"; on April 20 the royal governor of Virginia ordered the seizure of 20 kegs of powder at Williamsburg; the following night, citizens at Charles Town led by the new convert to resistance, William Henry Drayton, entered Hobcaw and Cochran's magazines and the State House. They carried off 1,600 pounds of powder, 800 guns, 200 cutlasses, flints, and other military stores. Alarmed at the theft of the King's stores, an act which constituted high treason, royal Lieutenant Governor William Bull asked the Commons

House of Assembly to investigate. Although prominent members of the House participated in the seizure of weapons, the Assembly reported back to Bull that they were unable to gain the necessary "intelligence" to determine who took the arms.

Events now tumbled crazily one upon another. In early May the news of Lexington and Concord reached Charles Town. At about the same time rumors spread that the British were planning to incite Indian attacks and slave rebellions across South Carolina. These reports were described as "causing the boiling of much blood." A royal official hurriedly dispatched a report to his London government warning that there was much talk in Charles Town of "storming Boston and destroying the British troops" there.

The call went out for the Provincial Congress to reconvene at Charles Town on June 1. When the Congress met, it quickly ordered the raising of three regiments, authorized funds for the defense of South Carolina, and created a 13-member Council of Safety. The radicals captured the meeting. They drafted a document known as the "Association" by which it was unanimously agreed that the representatives should be prepared to "go forth and sacrifice [their] lives and fortunes against every foe" in defense of liberty. Citizens who refused to sign the "Association" were to be treated as enemies. Henry Laurens, who was elected president of the Congress, opposed the growing tar and feather mentality. But moderate voices were drowned out by the sounds of violence. A crown officer reported that "a numerous body of the low and ignorant" led by "a few incendiaries and some hotheaded young men of fortune" were bent on "desperate measures." His assessment was accurate. One of the "most violent incendiaries in the Province" was William Henry Drayton.

Drayton and members of the Committee of Safety prowled the streets during the summer seeking signers to the "Association" and identifying those "inimical to the Liberties of America." Royal officials and crown sympathizers were dragged before the Committee, disarmed, and confined to the town. William Wragg, an influential planter considered dangerous to the American cause, was restricted to his plantation and later banished. After leaving the colony, he was shipwrecked and drowned. Two avowed loyalists to the crown were taken by a mob, stripped, tarred and feathered, and carted through the streets as an example to others. In early August when a British soldier, George Walker, refused "to drink damnation" to the King, an angry crowd jostled him through the streets. Armed with tar and feathers, the mob stopped before the home of one royal official and tossed a bag of feathers onto his balcony. The crowd shouted that he should "take care of it 'til his turn came." The mob pushed and shoved Walker along Broad Street to the Exchange Building. Here a kangaroo court "condemned" him for being "a Tory and an enemy to the country." He was sentenced to be "stripped naked, tarred and feathered all over his body."

Amazingly Walker lived to report that the sentence was carried out. He was pelted with rocks, doused repeatedly with water, and thrown into the Cooper River. By chance a passing boat picked him up, saving him from certain drowning. Walker lost an eye from the hot tar and sustained two broken ribs. A loyalist sympathizer in Charles Town declared that the King's friends are despondent, "expecting every moment to be drove from their occupations, and homes and plundered of all they have."

Before the summer ended, a free Negro, Thomas Jeremiah, charged with inciting slave rebellions, was con-

Courtesy Carolina Art Association/Gibbes Museum of
Captain Barnard Elliott

victed on hearsay evidence and executed. Ironically, slaves who parroted the cries of "liberty" which they heard in Charles Town's streets were quickly clapped into confinement.

In the late summer Charles Town "incendiaries" learned that local royal officials were urging Loyalists in the backcountry to join forces with regular troops imminently expected to arrive aboard British ships-of-war. Faced with these threats, the Council of Safety decided that British garrisoned Fort Johnson must be taken. Guarding the southeastern entrance to the harbor, it was considered crucial to the town's defenses. The newly elected officers of South Carolina's Army, yet to be raised, were given the mission.

On the evening of September 14, 1775, the town's ranking officer, Colonel William Moultrie, ordered Captains Charles Cotesworth Pinckney, Barnard Elliott, and Francis Marion to prepare their recently recruited com-

Courtesy Carolina Art Association/Gibbes Museum of Art

Major General William Moultrie

panies for action. Near midnight a strike force of 150 men assembled at Gadsden's wharf on the Cooper. Here officers and men embarked on two packets. Once underway Colonel Isaac Mott called the officers together to discuss the plan of attack.

Near dawn the boats bumped ashore on James Island. Hoping to surprise the garrison, the troops quickly spilled out of the boats and sprinted toward their objective. At any moment they anticipated drawing fire from the fort. Rushing through the unguarded gates, they were amazed to find the fort abandoned. British officials evidently had learned of the assault only hours before and had ordered the garrison aboard British ships in the harbor.

Nevertheless, the strategically located fort was in American hands. A blue flag bearing a silver crescent designed by Colonel Moultrie soon was raised over the fort. It was the first Patriot flag flown in South Carolina. With the addition of a palmetto tree after the Battle of Sullivan's Island less than a year later, it became the official flag of the State of South Carolina.

On the same day that Fort Johnson was occupied, royal Governor Lord William Campbell fled his lower Meeting Street residence and was rowed out to the British sloop-of-war *Tamar*. Royal government had ended in South Carolina.

Fearing that the *Tamar*, the *Cherokee*, and other British warships might attempt an assault on the town, the newly seated Provincial Congress ordered the blockade of main channels to the harbor. It is not surprising that the new president of the Congress, the firebrand William Henry Drayton, took direct command. Although a contemporary sneered that Drayton "was no sailor, and did not know any one rope from another," he personally supervised the scuttling of four rotting hulks in the Hog Island Channel from the deck of the armed schooner *Defence* on the afternoon of November 11. The captain of the 16-gun *Tamar* immediately opened fire on the hulks. No doubt Drayton was delighted. He had hoped to draw hostile fire to rally the moderates in the Provincial Congress to more aggressive action. He ordered his nine-pounder guns to reply. At dark, both sides ceased firing, but at dawn the following day the *Tamar*, now joined by the *Cherokee*, began firing broadsides, to which the *Defence* again responded.

Cannon fire booming across the harbor drew hundreds of citizens. Crowding along Bay Street they cheered the exchange. When the *Defence* broke off the engagement around 7 o'clock in the morning and returned to the city wharves, citizens greeted her with loud "huzzas." There were no casualties on either side despite the exchange of some 200 cannon balls. Both sides had com-

Courtesy South Carolina Historical Society

Colonel William Moultrie's Flag

mitted acts of war. The first shots of the Revolution in South Carolina had been fired.

The overt acts of war played into the hands of the "hot-headed young men of Fortune" like Drayton. So too did the presence of the British warships which continued to lurk off Charles Town's bar. Throughout the fall and into early 1776 troops were recruited and drilled, batteries erected, schooners outfitted for coastal defense, and provisions and arms gathered.

Fears of a British bombardment or invasion continued to send tremors through the town. Many citizens moved to the countryside. The Reverend Oliver Hart noted in his diary in the early fall: "I with my whole family and effects fled from Chas. Town for fear of the Enemy." In late November, Eliza Lucas Pinckney had made plans to leave town for a plantation on the Ashepoo if an attack

Courtesy Vic Brandt, Charleston, S. C.

The Sloop Defence

came. Already, she wrote, "almost all the Women, and many hundred Men have left town." But she agonized over having to flee, leaving her male relatives behind and perhaps "this poor unhappy Town, devoted to the Flames." Some removed their furniture to the country, but returned to the town to defend it. Henry Laurens assured his son John on November 26, 1775, "I am in good health, sitting in a House stripped of its furniture & in danger of being knocked down in a very few days by Cannon Ball." In December, Laurens wrote that the town remained "threatened every hour with a cannonade from four ships, besides small craft."

By the early part of 1776 even more people had fled the city. One resident who remained wrote: "Half the best Houses were empty." Some of these homes belonged to Loyalists who had been forced to leave. As the raw recruits streamed into Charles Town from the countryside, they moved into some houses and "destroyed & even burnt as firewood such furniture as remained." Charles Town began to resemble an armed camp.

Enlisted by recruiting officers armed with soft words, "hard money and strong drink," the volunteers came in. They had to be housed, fed, clothed, and whipped into combat-ready troops by the officers of South Carolina's army gathering at Charles Town. An English visitor about this time observed that the officers "are all people of property and cut a pretty good appearance having handsome uniforms." However, the enlisted men "make a worse figure than the Train Bands of London." Colonel Moultrie in command of the First and Second Regiments at Charles Town adopted a uniform for the units of blue coats, waist coats, and breeches trimmed in scarlet. Completing the outfit was a black felt hat, the brim trimmed off in back and up-turned in front. A silver crescent was sewn to the front part of the headpiece. The troops were provided with salt pork, rice, bread, vinegar, salt and pepper, rum, and sometimes "fresh provisions."

Throughout the fall and into early 1776 officers like Captain, later Colonel, Charles Cotesworth Pinckney tried to make soliders of the recruits. It was a difficult task for the future two-time candidate for President of the United States. Holding duty, honor, and service sacred, Pinckney told his men that "the most glorious of all characters" was the "good soldier." He drilled them in the manual of arms, he marched them, and he chided them on their personal habits. When reports reached him that his soldiers were stealing civilian property, he scolded them. Since the soldiers were guardians of South Carolina property, stealing, he told his troops, was an "infamous breach of trust reposed" in the soldiers by the citizens. Pinckney was constantly dressing down his men for their "drunkenness and rioting," and he told them that their "very ample pay" was not given for getting soused.

Even after his regiment was recognized as one of the best dressed and best drilled units in South Carolina, Pinckney had his problems. As he prepared to move the First Regiment from Fort Johnson to Sullivan's Island in 1776, he was unable to account for many of his men. He suspected that some were "still lurking in the Dram shops" of Charles Town. He thought that "about eighty" had "deserted."

As the efforts went on to whip the recruits into soldiers, the physical defenses of the town were also improved. At Fort Johnson repairs were made and new batteries mounted; earthworks were constructed and cannons implaced on Haddrell's Point near Mount Pleasant; in early 1776 the Council of Safety ordered the building of

Courtesy the National Portrait Gallery, Smithsonian Institution
Captain Charles Cotesworth Pinckney

"a strong fort and battery" on Sullivan's Island "for defending the channel and harbor of Charles Town."

Artisans of the town were well paid for their work on the batteries. Gangs of slaves were recruited for the heavy labor. Negroes were also organized into fire brigades. Supplied with hoses, axes, ropes, and ladders, they were stationed at strategic points about the town and were ordered to be ready at a moment's notice to extinguish any fires started by bombardments.

Elaborate signals were designed to alert the town to approaching British vessels. If sails were sighted on the horizon, pennants were to be raised and flown above Fort Johnson and the embattlement under construction on Sullivan's Island. By November patrols ranged along the seacoast from George Town to Haddrell's Point "to repel the Landing of men from British vessels."

At the same time the South Carolina navy was being born. By early 1776 the schooners *Polly* and *Defence,* the brigantine *Comet,* and the ships *Betsy* and *Prosper* had been converted and armed to patrol off Charles Town. Although the latter ship's conversion to a fighting vessel was personally and lovingly supervised by the firebrand Drayton, she never saw service at sea. The *Prosper* lacked the maneuverability required of fighting ships; it leaked and nearly sank when heavy guns were mounted aboard.

When word reached Christopher Gadsden at Philadelphia where he was attending the Second Continental Congress that Charles Town was threatened by British ships, he rushed back to South Carolina. The volatile, rash, and ambitious Gadsden saw himself at the head of an army defending his native ground. His colleague at Philadelphia, Thomas Lynch, remarked: "Gadsden is gone home to command our troops, God save them."

By the time Gadsden arrived, Charles Town was no longer under the immediate threat of a British bombardment. He found South Carolina's Second Provincial Congress deep in debate over the drafting of a constitution. The representatives had been instructed by the Continental Congress to establish a government, temporarily at least, which could function independently of the crown.

In early February, 1776, Gadsden appeared before the representatives meeting at the State House in Charles

Courtesy South Carolina Historical Society

Christopher Gadsden's Flag

Town. With him he brought a copy of Thomas Paine's *Common Sense* calling for independence from England, his own zeal for "absolute independence," and a yellow banner bearing a coiled rattlesnake under which was inscribed the words: "Don't Tread On Me." It was a duplicate of the flag Gadsden had designed as the personal standard for the commander of the American Navy. Gadsden's zeal for "absolute independence" shocked the more moderate Carolinians. But he did serve on a committee with the lowcountry's social and political elite — John Rutledge, Henry Laurens, Rawlins Lowndes, Henry Middleton, and Thomas Lynch, Jr. — who hammered out a temporary basis for a government for South Carolina. On March 26, 1776, the Second

Provincial Congress ratified the new constitution. John Rutledge was elected president and became the state's first chief executive. South Carolina became the first colony in the South to adopt a constitution, and would be the second to do so among the emerging new nation of states.

Courtesy Carolina Art Association/Gibbes Museum of Art

Thomas Lynch, Jr.

Yet even by mid-1776, several months after England had declared the Colonies to be in a state of rebellion, after blood had been spilled in Massachusetts, and acts of war had been committed in South Carolina, perhaps only two men among the lowcountry elite advocated independence — Christopher Gadsden and William Henry Drayton. While reluctant rebels like Henry Laurens found Paine's *Common Sense* full of indecent "expressions" toward the crown, Gadsden and Drayton praised it. The latter by late April, 1776, was telling the citizens of Charles Town: "The Almighty created America to be independent of Britain. Let us beware of the impiety of being backward to act as instruments in the Almighty hand." Drayton's interpretation of the Divine Will did not sway many South Carolinians to strike for independence. But the British attack near Charles Town in June, 1776, did.

At British Headquarters in Boston early in 1776, General Sir William Howe, commander-in-chief of British forces in America since October, 1775, ordered his second in command, General Sir Henry Clinton, to lead the initial campaign against the South. With a small force Clinton sailed from Boston harbor in January. At the same time, a larger naval and military expedition led by Sir Peter Parker and gathering in English waters was directed to proceed to stations off the North Carolina coast and join with Clinton's forces. Strategists in the London government and General Howe aimed at establishing a temporary base of operations in the South. They believed that such a show of force would encourage American Loyalists to rally to the King's cause.

Sailing southward along the coast, Clinton, having gathered intelligence indicating that the Loyalists were ready to rise in North Carolina, decided to establish a headquarters at Cape Fear. But when he arrived in March, 1776, he was greeted with bad news. A Loyalist

Sir Henry Clinton

force had been smashed in a clash with rebels at Moore's Creek Bridge two weeks earlier, and there was no sign of Admiral Peter Parker's expedition. Not until early May did Parker's long-delayed fleet arrive.

After conferring, Clinton and Parker considered proceeding toward Charles Town, but first they sent a reconnaissance team of two junior officers southward. In late May they reported back that Sullivan's Island at the mouth of Charles Town's harbor was defended by a

Courtesy South Carolina Historical Society

Sir Peter Parker

vulnerable, unfinished fortification. Encouraged by this report, and eager to launch the plan of London strategists and General Howe somewhere, Clinton and Parker ordered an immediate attack designed to take and hold Sullivan's Island.

The logic of this plan seems muddled. A strike at Charles Town itself and its capture would have demonstrated a greater show of strength and offered Loyalists a more easily accessible rallying point than remote Sullivan's Island. If the assault on the island succeeded and a base of operations established, where would supplies for a garrison be secured? Also the island was of little strategic value. It was far distant from the main theatres of the war in the North. And once their plan was

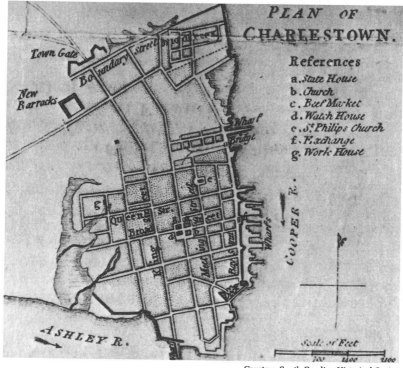

Courtesy South Carolina Historical Society

Charles Town, 1776
(from a map made in 1776)

launched, Clinton and Parker piled blunder on blunder. However, if their mission had aimed at only terrifying lowcountry citizens, they would have succeeded grandly. Since residents of Charles Town were unaware of the limited objectives of the British offensive, word of an approaching armada sent tremors through the town.

On May 31, cries of "British sails" swept through the streets of South Carolina's capital. Alarms were fired, and signal pennants were raised over the fortifications. Throughout the next 48 hours civilians and military men alike watched with growing apprehensions as an armada assembled off the bar. From Fort Johnson on James Island Captain Thomas Pinckney was astonished to see "more than 40 vessels of *all sorts*, sloops, schooners etc." Transports carrying over 3,000 British troops and supply ships were supported by numerous warships. Two heavy frigates, the *Bristol* and the *Experiment,* mounted 50 guns; six lighter frigates including the *Soleby, D'Active, Actaeon,* and *Syren,* carried 28 guns each while the frigate *Friendship* displayed 26 and the *Sphynx* 20. Another vessel, the *Thunderbomb,* was equipped to throw mortars. One resident in anguish noted that the armada seemed "to cover the sea" off Charles Town.

Initially, panic engulfed the town. An observer wrote that men began "running about looking for horses, carriages and boats to send their families into the country." Mrs. Ann Manigault entered in her diary: "I went up to Goosecreek in a Waggon, as the British Men of War were coming in." The newspaper presses were dismantled and carried from the town. To prevent the desertion of troops, Colonel Moultrie ordered sentinels stationed at all arteries leading out of town. The male civilians were assembled and urged to "brandish the pick-axe and spade as well as the sword in defense of their country." One resident saw "examples immediately made, *in terrorem,*" of those exhibiting "any disinclination to act." The few remaining crown officials were seized and confined. President of the Provincial Congress, John Rutledge, sent messengers flying into the hinterland on horseback to summon the militia. He alerted the one-time professional British Army officer, Major General

Charles Lee, now the American commander-in-chief of the Southern Department with headquarters near Wilmington, of the impending attack and urged him to march his force to Charles Town. "For God's sake," Rutledge implored, "lose not a moment." Lee immediately ordered a quick march southward.

Believing that the British objective was the town, Rutledge ordered its defenses strengthened and new ones rushed to completion. Relying on the fortifications ringing the harbor to prevent the British fleet from swinging close by the town, soldiers and conscripted slaves sweated side by side to improve the works at Fort Johnson and to build a new 12-gun redoubt nearby; at Haddrell's Point near Mount Pleasant additional trenches were dug; and at the northern end of the harbor near the southern tip of Sullivan's Island prodigious efforts were made to complete the 20-foot-high, double-walled fort of palmetto logs encircled by a ditch while artillery crews mounted some 20 cannons.

Faced with a critical shortage of ammunition, Rutledge directed slaves to strip lead ornaments from buildings for melting down into bullets. Negroes were stationed around the town to fight fires and sent to the fortified points to assist in the positioning and loading of cannons.

The officers and men of Charles Town's garrisons waited for the assault to begin. One defender told his brother on June 7: "We are preparing to make the most vigorous resistance in our power." Another, perhaps thinking of the battle that surely had to come, wrote to his wife: "Kiss my little angel Nancy, tell her, her Papa is ever thinking of her. Kiss little William that darling of us both, and tell him how his Papa loves him and that he must not forget his Papa." Captain Thomas Pinckney, young and full of bravado, wrote his sister from Fort

Johnson on June 5 and again on June 9. He stressed that the 650 defenders of the fort were "very cheerful" and intended to "give a very good account" of themselves if the British "shall be hardy enough to attack us."

But the British delayed, and foul weather blew up. General Clinton and Admiral Parker had committed their first blunder after launching the already illogical plan. Time was on the side of the Americans not the British. Defensive preparations were hurried forward in town and at the fortifications, and the country militia came "flocking" in. The arrival of General Lee and his several hundred Continentals bolstered both the morale and troop strength of the defenders. Captain Thomas Pinckney was encouraged by General Lee's arrival and described him as having "a great deal of the gentleman in his appearance tho' homely." Colonel William Moultrie believed that the presence of the one-time British Army officer "was equal to a reinforcement of 1,000 men." John Rutledge immediately delegated to Lee the authority to command the forces at Charles Town, now grown to over 6,000.

Critical of the defensive posture of the town, General Lee ordered the barricading of streets and the razing of buildings near the wharves to allow newly mounted cannons a wider angle of fire. Lee let it be known that he was "horrified" that the Carolinians were relying on the unfinished Sullivan's Island fort to protect the northern approach to the town. He called the fortification a "slaughter pen" for the Americans defending there. On June 22 Lee met with President Rutledge and his advisors and urged them to evacuate the island fort. Rutledge refused. He supported Colonel Moultrie who insisted that he and his men could repel any attack by land and sea. Even if a British cannonade leveled the fort, Moultrie asserted, "we will lay behind the ruins and prevent their men from landing."

General Lee accepted the decision. He sought now to make the best of what he still believed to be a desperate situation. He rushed gangs of slaves to Sullivan's Island and personally supervised their efforts to complete the works at the northwest angle of the fortification. To protect the rear flank of Colonel Moultrie's nearly 400 defenders of the Second South Carolina Regiment, Lee stationed 780 riflemen and two field pieces under the command of Colonel William Thomson at the northern tip of the island. Already General Clinton was ashore on Long Island, today the Isle of Palms, massing 2,000 British regulars for an amphibious assault across Breach Inlet to the neighboring Sullivan's Island's northern end. Lee reduced the size of the garrison at Fort Johnson now commanded by the recently commissioned Colonel Christopher Gadsden. Long spoiling for a command and a fight, Gadsden had wrangled an appointment as commander of the First South Carolina Regiment. Fifteen hundred men under Lee's aide, Brigadier General John Armstrong, were dispatched to Haddrell's Point. Lee stationed the remaining 2,000 troops at fortified positions about the town. The Americans continued to wait.

The initial British plan of attack called for a coordinated land and sea assault on the Sullivan's Island fort. General Clinton would rush his massed troops on Long Island across Breach Inlet to Sullivan's Island's northern tip and then strike the defenders of the fort at the rear. At the same time Admiral Parker would commence the bombardment of the fort.

This strategy was shattered on June 18. To Clinton's "unspeakable mortification" Breach Inlet was discovered to be too deep to ford. He had underestimated the depth by five feet! Clinton's intelligence service had blundered. When Admiral Parker was so notified, he seemed to imply to Clinton that his ships alone were equal to the task at hand; Parker told Clinton to do the best he could when the naval bombardment began. Now Clinton's quartermasters scurried to secure all the long boats they could find. The troops would have to be ferried across Breach Inlet. Coordination between the army and navy was breaking down.

On the morning of June 28 before a favorable breeze and on a rising tide, Admiral Parker ordered his ships into action. At least he had managed to catch Clinton and his troops completely by surprise. They had received no notice of the impending attack. Hurriedly directing his troops into the few long boats available to him, Clinton attempted to support the fleet's maneuver.

Across Breach Inlet, entrenched behind redoubts, sandhills, and scrub myrtle bushes, Colonel Thomson's troops watched. The British regulars seemed close enough to shake hands with. When it appeared that the redcoats were going to attempt a crossing, Thomson's troops opened a murderous fire with field pieces and small arms. Neutralized by tides, channel depths, and Thomson's fire, General Clinton and his army could only watch the naval bombardment getting underway.

Inside the fortification at the opposite end of Sullivan's Island the defenders also observed Admiral Parker's vessels bearing down on the fort. At "ten minutes before eleven o'clock" an officer watched a shell thrown by the *Thunderbomb* arch over the fort. The bombardment had begun.

Stationing the *Thunderbomb* and his heavier ships about 600 yards off the island to cannonade the fort, Admiral Parker ordered the three frigates *Syren*, *Sphynx*, and *Actaeon* to run downchannel past the embattlement and bring their starboard broadsides to bear on the unfinished northwest side. Almost immediately

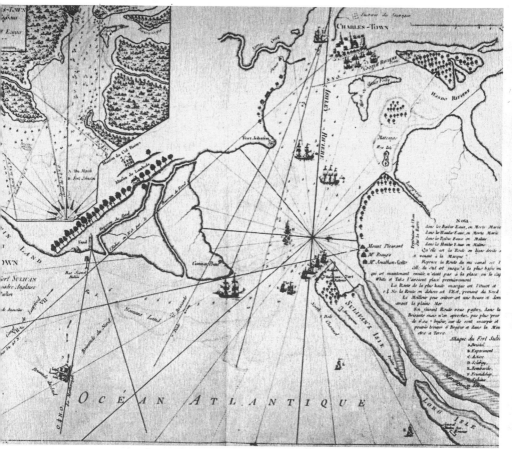

Courtesy Carolina Art Association/Gibbes Museum of Art

A French Officer's Map of the British Attack on
Sullivan's Island, 1776

the three frigates ran aground on shoals. Helpless, they
became "sitting ducks" for gunners in the fort. The
heavier ships, however, continued to bombard the fortification. Although the spongy palmetto logs easily
absorbed the shot, numerous rounds fell among the
defenders inside. "Clouds of smoke curled over our
heads," the cannon sounded like "one continual blaze
and roar," Colonel Moultrie observed. He ordered "grog
in fire-buckets" passed among the defenders who responded "very heartily."

Behind the palmetto logs Dr. Peter Fayssoux had his
hands full. "A mulatto waiting boy" was struck;
"Lieutenant Henry Gray received a swivel ball in his
breast"; Lieutenant Thomas Hall's cheek was smashed

Courtesy South Carolina Historical Society

A British View of the Attack on Sullivan's Island

Courtesy South Carolina Historical Society

An Artist's View of the Action from within the Fort
(from *Harper's Weekly*, June, 1858)

by a splinter; a sergeant fell mortally wounded, his "stomach and bowels shot away by a cannon ball." Before he died several comrades heard him cry: "Fight on my brave boys, don't let liberty expire with me today." When a ball smashed the flag staff over the fort, Sergeant William Jasper, shouting, "don't let us fight without a color," grabbed a sponge staff, hastily tied the flag to it, leaped atop the bastion, and stuck the staff into a merlon. The garrison roared three long cheers.

Watching the cannon duel from across the harbor at Fort Johnson, Colonel Gadsden, Captain Thomas Pinckney, and their men moaned at being only spectators. "Every man," Pinckney declared, "longed earnestly to have been there" to share the "honor and danger with their fellow soldiers."

Running low on powder and shot, Colonel Moultrie instructed his gunners to wait for the cannon smoke to lift around the British ships and to aim well in returning

Courtesy Carolina Art Association/Gibbes Museum of Art
Sergeant Jasper Replacing the Colors
(Currier and Ives)

fire. The defenders obeyed their orders to the letter. Observers on both sides saw the "main and mizen mast shot away" on Parker's flagship the *Bristol*. Its quarter-deck was twice cleared of every man by fire from the fort; its captain, John Morris, was killed, and Parker himself twice wounded. The *Experiment* also suffered heavy damage in "hull and rigging" and lost its captain, Alexander Scott, and over 20 seamen. A lieutenant and six men were killed aboard the *D'Active*, and the *Soleby* also took heavy casualties.

Near dusk cannon fire from both ships and fort became sporadic. At nightfall it ceased. Parker signaled his ships to move beyond range of the American guns. On a rising tide he refloated two of his grounded frigates; unable to move the *Actaeon*, he ordered her scuttled. The British ships were so badly battered, with scores of dead and dying littered about the decks, that further action was out of the question.

"Thus," a British officer wrote, was "the Invincible British Navy defeated by a Battery which was supposed would not have stood one Broadside." A crown official who had watched the engagement from Charles Town bitterly remarked: "Had the conduct of the commanders equaled the courage of their men we should not have occasion to lament so disgraceful a disaster."

When news of the outcome of the battle became apparent in Charles Town, the inhabitants were giddy with joy. The Reverend Oliver Hart believed divine providence had saved the town. He cried: "God appeared for us, and defeated our enemies." But to General Lee who rushed the news to General George Washington and the Continental Congress, the victory was the result of "the cool courage" of the "gallant defenders." He praised the "noble" Thomson and Moultrie who deserved "eternal credit" for the victory.

On July 1, citizens of Charles Town sailed or rowed anything that would float to the island to salute the defenders. Standing well off the island were Admiral Parker's ships, their cannonball-pitted hulls, torn sails, and tangled rigging quite visible. Dignitaries reviewed the Second Carolina Regiment drawn up outside the battered, newly christened Fort Moultrie. General Lee praised their valor, President Rutledge presented his sword to Sergeant William Jasper, and the dark-eyed and dark-haired Susannah Elliott, recent bride of Major Barnard Elliott, gave the regiment two flags, one red and one blue. She praised their "gallant behavior" and told them to stand by the colors "as long as they wave in the air of liberty." On one flag Susannah had embroidered the Latin motto: *Vita Potior Libertas,* "Liberty is more to be desired than life."

After re-embarking General Clinton's troops from Long Island, Admiral Parker and his fleet lingered off Charles Town licking their wounds. Knowing that the British were suffering from a lack of fresh food, General Lee, displaying the courtesy of eighteenth-century warriors, sent Clinton a quantity of fruit and vegetables. In return Clinton sent Lee a cask of port and some English cheese. Then in late July the last sails of the battered British fleet dropped beyond the horizon off Charles Town.

Bound for New York to join the main British Army, Clinton and Parker would have liked to have left their blunders behind them. But an American ballad-maker soon broadcast to the world the comedy of errors off the Southern port city. Putting the whole affair into Admiral Sir Peter Parker's mouth, the words of the ballad ran:

> Bold Clinton by land
> Did quietly stand
> While I made a thundering clatter;
> But the channel was deep,

So he only could peep,
And not venture over the water.
De'el take 'em, their shot
Came so swift and so hot,
And the cowardly dogs stood so stiff, sirs!
That I put ship about,
And was glad to get out,
Or they would not have left me a skiff, sirs!
Now bold as a Turk
I proceed to New York,
Where with Clinton and Howe you may find me.
I've wind in my tail
And am hoisting my sail,
To leave Sullivan's Island behind me.

Scarcely had the echoes of the roar of cannonading near Charles Town rolled away when the Continental Congress at Philadelphia adopted a Declaration of Independence from England. The British attack on Sullivan's Island and the Patriots' blood spilled there made the decision easier for lowcountry citizens to accept. The casualties had been among their personal friends. Dr. Peter Fayssoux, who had cut and patched all day behind the palmetto logs, became an "irreconcilable" for independence. The friends of one artisan defender consecrated the blood he had spilled by singing to the tune of "Yankee Doodle":

The First of June the British Fleet
Appear'd off Charles Town harbour;
The Twenty-eight attack'd the fort,
And wounded Young the barber.

Christopher Gadsden and William Henry Drayton, who had long warned that "Americans can not leave it in the power of the British rulers to injure them," warmly embraced the strike for independence. But some lowcountry leaders like John Rutledge and Charles Pinckney thought the move for independence was premature. Still others absolutely refused to barter the security and prosperity they enjoyed under the crown and the sentimental attachment to England and King for a struggle which might lead only to anarchy. Lowcountry citizens did not stand united on the decision for independence.

On August 5, 1776, the Declaration of Independence was proclaimed publicly in Charles Town. Near 1 o'clock it was first read before the leading military and civilian officials and the town militia standing under arms on Broad Street. The procession then marched slowly east down Broad Street to the Exchange where the words were read again:

> When, in the course of human events,
> it becomes necessary for one people
> to dissolve the political bonds which
> have connected them with another . . .
> they should declare the causes which
> impel them to the separation. . . .

The crowd cheered, and cannons boomed salutes along the Cooper. The Presbyterian pastor William Tennent observed: "No event seemed to diffuse more general Satisfaction among the People." But Henry Laurens wrote that he "wept that day and felt much . . . pain." He felt like a dutiful son "thrust by the hand of violence out of his father's house." With hope and trepidation he looked forward to "a new world," one in which "God only knows what sort of a world it will be." But now he was willing to sacrifice "his crops, land, and Life, in preference to sacrificing Liberty." Unlike other lowcountry elite, Laurens believed also that the logic of a revolution for liberty should include liberty for black slaves. So too did his son John Laurens.

With the ardor and idealism of youth, the younger Laurens unequivocally welcomed independence. He exclaimed that "the sword of State is unsheath'd and borne in a Declaration of War against Geo. 3d." With equal bravado young William Bull, Jr., of Charles Town celebrated the virtuous strike for independence and wrote a friend in England on August 13: "All the troops both foreign and domestic that Great Britain can send will not be able to hurt America. She bids degenerate Britain defiance."

But loyalty to the crown also coursed through Charles Town in the summer of 1776. The minister of St. Michael's Church, the Reverend Robert Cooper, offered prayers from his pulpit for the King during July. Only public pressures on the vestry led to Cooper's dismissal. He soon departed for England where he received a pension as a Loyalist. The die was now officially cast. In the new State of South Carolina, one had to choose between Patriot or Loyalist.

Severance of ties with England prompted a call for a new state constitution. Shortly after the Legislature convened at Charles Town in September, 1776, a committee was appointed to draft the document. The two men who had so zealously prodded South Carolina to cut its ties with the English government, Gadsden and Drayton. now worked "feverishly" to create the foundation of the new government. But legislative delays and sectional selfishness between lowcountry and backcountry delayed presentation of the constitution to the Assembly for debate and passage until early March, 1778.

Essentially a conservative document, it proclaimed the state's independence and provided for a governor and a popularly elected two-house legislature. Gadsden, Drayton, and their radical allies did secure the inclusion of two democratic features — a bill of rights and divestiture of the aristocratic Anglican Church of public financial support.

Too conservative for some, the new constitution was too liberal for others. Several of the planter elite were so disturbed by the more democratic features of the constitution that they denounced Gadsden as a madman. Surprising to all was President John Rutledge's resignation before the House on March 5 in protest of the new constitution. A member of the Assembly wrote: "It was not expected. We stood amazed looking at one another."

The main reason compelling Rutledge to resign was the provision in the constitution declaring the state's independence from England. Even at this late date some conservatives hoped for reconciliation. But Gadsden from the floor of the Assembly, and Henry Laurens and William Henry Drayton from their seats in the Continental Congress, denounced Rutledge's action. A little more than a year later the radical cause would lose one of its most brilliant firebrands, William Henry Drayton. He would die of a "putrid fever" at Philadelphia, far from his native lowcountry soil.

Upon Rutledge's resignation, the radicals attempted to hoist their leader Gadsden to the governorship under the new constitution. The move failed by a vote of 54 to 48; the moderate Rawlins Lowndes was elected. Nearly as reluctant a revolutionary as Rutledge, Lowndes already was known to the radicals as "the great procrastinator." To shelve the troublesome Gadsden and salve the feelings of the firebrands, the Assembly elected him lieutenant governor. Initially outraged at being, as Gadsden put it, "got out of the way," he soon came to worry over the continuing agitation which ironically he had helped unloose years before.

On March 28, 1776, the Legislature passed a surprisingly punitive act requiring all citizens over 16 to take an oath of loyalty to the "free, independent, and sovereign state" of South Carolina. In doing so citizens had to renounce their allegiance to the crown and vow to defend the state against invasion by the armies of George III. Anyone refusing to pledge his loyalty could neither hold office nor transact business in the state.

Unwilling to take such an oath, several dozen prominent, mainly middle aged, professional men and merchants immediately made plans to sail from Charles Town for Florida, British-occupied New York, the West Indies, or England. Other Loyalists and their families trickled out of town during the late spring. However, a group calling themselves the "Friends of the British Government" refused to either leave or take the test oath despite the threats of Charles Town bully-boys, the one-time followers of Gadsden.

The possibility of violence and the physical problem of enforcing the oath prompted Governor Lowndes to issue a proclamation in early June extending the date for taking the pledge. The proclamation infuriated the Charles Town radicals. A resident wrote: "The day it was published the people assembled, ringing Bells, & were very uneasy." On June 5 a mob precipitated a riot when the local sheriff attempted to read the proclamation. Fearing "ruin to their liberties," the crowd seized the document and returned it to Governor Lowndes with threats of impeachment. A deputation representing the radicals, Doctor John Budd, Lawyer Joshua Ward, and Edwin Lightwood, a merchant, sought to see Lowndes but were intercepted by the new Lieutenant Governor Christopher Gadsden on the State House steps. Gadsden saw that they were excited and angry. And in defending the proclamation he came close to blows with the lawyer Ward. Gadsden's support of Governor Lowndes "has much displeased the people & made him very unpopular," a Charles Town citizen wrote.

The long-time advocate of violent action against unpopular acts also was displeased and disappointed. The radical revolutionary was turning conservative. His own newly acquired power was being threatened by "mobocracy." Seeing the fury of a mob for the first time from the other side, Gadsden wrote a friend on June 8: "I am afraid we have too many amongst us [who] want to be running upon every Fancy to the Meeting of [the] Liberty Tree, a Disease amongst us far more dangerous than any thing that can arise from the whole present herd of Contemptible, exportable Tories."

Not only were the people showing a growing distrust of their old leaders now in new positions, but there was a rising spirit for vengeance against Loyalists. Soon refusals to pledge allegiance to the new state were met with banishment and confiscation of property. Civil war was threatening to engulf the lowcountry.

CHAPTER III

Charles Town Besieged

The actual din and smell of battle was not heard or scented in Charles Town for several years after the repulse of the British at Sullivan's Island. The English were concentrating their efforts in the northeast. However, indirectly the effects of the war being waged for independence were sharply felt by residents of the town.

Soaring prices and the scarcity of food plagued citizens of the lowcountry. Paper bills issued by the Continental Congress and the State of South Carolina to finance the war effort and largely unbacked by gold or silver soon caused rampant inflation. An item selling for a shilling in Charles Town in 1777 might cost 61 shillings by 1780. A member of the wealthy and powerful Manigault family at Charles Town agonized in March, 1777: "We have been greatly Distressed for want of many Necessarys of Life." A few months later a military officer trying to secure supplies at Charles Town wrote his superior: "We have had quite a lot of trouble to obtain [provisions] because of the cost. Everything is a thousand percent more expensive since the War." As prices of meat and grain soared, one resident of Charles Town complained in early 1778 that "worm eaten corn is now sold which, at other times, would be judged only fit for beasts."

For many planters of the lowcountry's main crops, rice and indigo, agriculture went from "bad to worse." By 1778 embargoes placed by the Continental Congress on both staples disrupted the normal channels of trade for the planters. Additionally the indigo farmer was plagued by the lack of money for capital investment in vats, drying sheds and wells, and such packaging materials as barrels and sacks. To prevent the possible loss of provisions to the American armies by export, the Continental Congress also prohibited the export of such items as corn, beef, pork, bacon, and livestock in June, 1778. Due to such measures the overseer of Henry Laurens' plantations wrote from Charles Town to wonder if "this years crop will bear your great Expenses."

Artisans and craftsmen of the town also suffered financially. Bricklayer and builder Timothy Crosby had to sell his property to meet his debts and obligations due to soaring costs. Richard Magrath the cabinetmaker was forced to go out of business because of "want of materials."

Adding to the financial plight of some artisans was the conflagration that swept through a part of the town on the night of January 15, 1778. Breaking out toward the eastern end of Broad Street near the intersection of Queen and Church Streets, the fire burned down to Stoll's Alley. Before it was extinguished, the fire consumed 248 dwellings and "twice that number of outhouses and stores." Some artisan establishments were destroyed. A citizen on the scene observed: "Many who a few hours before retired to their bed in affluence were now reduced to indigence." A visitor to the town reported that the fire "has made dreadful havoc having destroyed the precious trading part of it, and many elegant buildings."

Charles Town craftsmen experienced little relief from one of the main causes propelling them to support independence — the end of competition from their overseas rivals in London, Glasgow, Manchester, and other British cities. Wares from England by way of the Danish,

French, and Dutch West Indies continued to flow into Charles Town. They were imported by the many new merchants who were willing to take the great risk to make a great profit under the wartime conditions.

Some businessmen pursued profits in the exports of agricultural products despite the American-imposed embargo. From 1777-1780 indigo shipments out of the port town were sold in the Northern states, the West Indies, France, and Holland. Even an insurance company was formed at Charles Town in 1777 to encourage trade.

Out-of-state merchants who came to Charles Town to take advantage of the commercial activity there profited handsomely. Robert Morris of New Jersey, a wealthy merchant and America's secretary of finance during the Revolution, became a partner in the firm of Stacey Hepburn and Company formed for the sole purpose of exploiting business opportunities in South Carolina. Hepburn himself came to Charles Town in 1779 to invest in indigo, rice, "goods, hard money or landed property." In short, Hepburn was authorized by his partners to invest in anything that would turn a profit.

Purchasing real estate, trading vessels, and thousands of pounds of indigo which he shipped out of Charles Town, Hepburn shrewdly carried out his instructions. When he departed the port town under threat of British invasion in 1780, Hepburn had reaped for the firm profits of about $60,000 in gold and silver. The lucrative wartime trade flowing in and out of Charles Town like the tide produced fortunes for a few.

Garrison life for the officers and men at Charles Town settled into a dull routine when the threat of a British invasion evaporated after 1776. The excitement of rallying round the colors was gone for many "summer soldiers and sunshine patriots." But low pay, poor food and quarters, and the desire to rejoin families and friends also led to low morale, unsoldierly conduct, and desertions; some of these same factors contributed to fewer enlistments although recruiting for South Carolina's regiments was stepped up.

By early 1777, Continental General Robert Howe, a North Carolinian, commanded the troops at Charles Town and throughout the South. On garrison duty at Fort Moultrie, Fort Johnson, Haddrell's Point, and within the town were elements of the First, Second, and Fifth South Carolina Regiments. Troops fit for duty never numbered above 600. In the town, soldiers maintained regular guard mounts at the Cumberland Street Magazine, their barracks, the General Hospital, Exchange Building, the State House, General Howe's Headquarters, Paul Pritchard's Ship Yard on Hobcaw Point, and batteries along the Cooper River.

Commanding these units with Howe, but subordinate to him, were the recently promoted Brigadier Generals William Moultrie and Christopher Gadsden. The latter, true to his ambitious and rash nature, soon became embroiled in a controversy with General Howe. Probably jealous of Howe's position and coveting his command, Gadsden challenged Howe to a duel. He permitted Howe to shoot first, and when his bullet went wild, Gadsden fired his own pistol into the air. Honor was assuaged all round, but Gadsden soon resigned his commission.

Persistent failures to augment the troop strength of the regiments at Charles Town worried Captain Thomas Pinckney. In early 1777 he wrote his sister: "I am much chagrined at the bad success we have met with in recruiting." Into 1778 the regiments remained at only half-strength. John Gervais, the overseer of Henry

Laurens' plantations, wrote from Charles Town that "it is difficult to fill them, when the Inhabitants don't incline to enlist for Soliders." "But," he added, "we are in hopes to fill them by a Vagrant Act." This measure passed the South Carolina Legislature in March, 1778. The act ordered the immediate enlistment of all "idle men, beggars, strolling or straggling persons" and deer-killing night hunters as privates in South Carolina's regiments. Persons voluntarily enlisting were offered 100 acres of land in South Carolina in addition to the 100 acres offered by the Continental Congress. Sizeable bounties were subsequently paid to "all recruits physically fit, having no sore legs, not less than 5 ft. 3 in. height, nor over forty-five years of age."

Despite such arbitrary measures and attractive inducements, troop strength remained down. A French official at Charles Town in late 1778 observed that the garrison numbered only 600 men, and these were "recruited with some difficulty." He also noted that the "troops were in a rather bad state both as regards dress and discipline, most of them being poorly armed and drilled."

The "rabble in arms" at Charles Town were neither well cared for nor well quartered. In the winter months they suffered from lack of blankets and fuel; in the summer and early fall they sweltered in the heat and fell victim to lowcountry fevers and diseases. To escape from these conditions and their dreary routines, the young, raw recruits gambled, got drunk, quarreled, and played pranks. They stole the officers' linen shirts and silk stockings from the laundry and fruit from the officers' tables, insulted the garrison chaplain, taunted citizens into fistfights, and fired salvos from the barracks windows at odd hours of the morning and night.

Constantly faced with such outbursts, General Howe and his officers constantly admonished the troops on their behavior, appearance, and dress. Orders forbade them to enter Charles Town's "dram shops," to eschew "drunkenness and disorderly behavior," to refrain from gambling, and to appear "powdered and clean dressed." The soldiers were commanded to shave three times weekly, ordered not to sleep in their clothes, and to avoid an "effeminate length of hair" by keeping it cut short. Colonel Francis Marion had a particular attitude toward hair. At Charles Town about this time, Marion ordered men of his regiment who did not cut their hair to "have it plaited and tied up as they will not be allowed to appear with their hair down their backs and over their foreheads, and down their chins at the sides, which make them appear more like wild savages than soldiers."

General Howe frequently admonished his officers on their own personal behavior, and he was sometimes infuriated by their lack of attention to the troops under their command. He condemned his officers' dissipation and gambling, warning that gaming could "Bring Disgrace and Ruin upon" them. He also may have worried over Captain Thomas Pinckney's frequent parties for the ladies. Pinckney often urged his sister Horriott to come to town and "bring all the fine Girls you can muster along with you." Entice them by promising them "a Dance and as many kisses as they can carry away," he urged.

Despite Howe's efforts, by the end of 1777 he had made little progress in instilling a high regard for discipline and appearance among his soldiers. In a furious outburst during a meeting with his officers in November, Howe condemned "the slovenly, indecent, dirty manner in which the soldiers appeared." It was "inconsis-

Courtesy South Carolina Historical Society

Major Thomas Pinckney

tent with health, disgraceful to the Army, censurable at all times, and when on duty absolutely inexcusable." Howe complained that even sentries had been sent to his headquarters "with bare legs, long beards, hats flopped, and uncombed hair." He concluded by dressing down his officers for their repeated "inattention and negligence" toward their men. Yet the South Carolina militia continued to "reluctantly submit to martial discipline." Most of these men had grown up on farms and were used to their "freedom and independence." A contemporary observed that when given a command, the militiamen "sometime inquire 'whither they were going?' and 'how long they must stay?' "

In mid-1778, the Charles Town garrison received intelligence indicating that the British were planning to mount an offensive against the South. The report was accurate. When the British evacuated Philadelphia in June, 1778, their chief objective until the end of the war was the recovery of the Southern Colonies.

Suddenly faced with another potential invasion, the Patriots made hurried efforts to prepare for the defense of Charles Town. To whip recalcitrant troops into line, harsh punishments were meted out. Desertions led to courts martial.

In the spring, James Olliver, John McNamara, and James Harlock were convicted of desertion and sentenced "to Suffer death by being Shot." Lots were drawn among several companies to determine who would execute the prisoners. Henry Martin and James Thomas of the Second Regiment and Bartholemew McDonald of the First Regiment were also convicted of desertion, but received less than capital punishment. All three were "sentenced to receive 100 lashes on the bare back with the cat of 9 tails." During July and August other military courts at Charles Town handed down similar sentences. A minister present at an execution for desertion wrote that he walked with the prisoner to the spot where the sentence was to be carried out while "the drums muffled beat the dead March." He talked and prayed with the condemned and then watched as the "unhappy victim, blindfolded and on his knees, received the shot."

The London government shifted its military strategy in 1778 for several reasons. British commanders operating in the Northern states had failed to quickly quash the rebellion by forcing Washington into a climactic battle.

In fact, to the surprise of English officialdom, the reverse had happened. In the woods of upstate New York in late 1777, "Gentleman" General Johnny Burgoyne surrendered an army of 5,000. This British defeat at Saratoga prompted France to openly avow its support of the American cause and to enter the war as an effective American ally in February, 1778. Confronted by these facts, British civilian and military leaders sought a quick strike against the Southern states to shift the tide of war in their favor. They believed that success in the South would come from their capability of maintaining naval superiority off the coast and the flocking of Southern Loyalists to fight with the King's regular forces. The new southern strategy was entrusted to the general stymied at Sullivan's Island in 1776, but who had subsequently redeemed himself, Sir Henry Clinton. In early 1778 he had succeeded Sir William Howe as the British commander-in-chief in North America.

To ready the South for the British blow, the Continental Congress appointed the Massachusetts-born farmer, Major General Benjamin Lincoln, to take charge of the American forces in the South. Described as having a "fighter's heart as large as his massive stomach," Lincoln left Philadelphia for South Carolina in October, 1778. He had instructions from General Washington to plan for the defense of Charles Town "in case the Enemy should form a expedition against it." On December 4, Lincoln arrived in South Carolina's capital city and established his headquarters on Tradd Street.

General Lincoln faced the formidable task of raising a large army, providing it with equipment and supplies, and shoring up Charles Town's defenses. On December 19 he received sobering reports. There were "very few" men fit for duty, "very few stores" available in town or without, and of the six Continental field pieces at Charles Town none was in operating condition. He also

Courtesy South Carolina Historical Society
Major General Benjamin Lincoln

soon discovered that the military commanders at Charles Town were in "abject dependence on the civil authority." He could not get supplies or even "march the troops" without the consent of the Governor of South Carolina.

While Lincoln rushed to raise an army, General Clinton at New York ordered an assault on Savannah, Georgia, capital of the youngest and weakest of the Southern Colonies. After a short siege by 3,500 British regulars under Colonel Archibald Campbell the port town fell to the English on December 29, 1778. Campbell's forces were soon joined by 2,000 troops under General Augustine Prevost. Using Savannah as a base of operations, the British swiftly moved inland. By early 1779 most of Georgia was under their control. The quick reduction of the state encouraged General Prevost to launch an attack on its neighbor, South Carolina. His initial target lay just over 100 miles to the north of Savannah, the strategically located port of Charles Town.

South Carolina civilian leaders and residents of the town were shocked at the new threat from the south. Governor Rawlins Lowndes wrote from the Carolina capital on January 21, 1779: "Our situation is truly critical and without spirited and manly Exertions we shall be disgraced in the eyes of America, and dispersed by the Enemy." Calls went out to Congress and the countryside for troops to complement Lincoln's still small force at Charles Town.

Deciding to take the war to the British in Georgia, General Lincoln marched out of Charles Town in late January with several thousand ill-disciplined and ill-equipped militia. General Moultrie was left behind with 1,200 troops to defend the state.

By mid-April, as Lincoln's troops were poised to cross south of the Savannah River to cut the British supply lines, General Prevost saw the opportunity to strike the near defenseless capital of South Carolina. Crossing the Savannah in the opposite direction and skirting Lincoln's command, Prevost rushed toward Charles Town. Alerted to Prevost's plan, General Moultrie raced to the defense of the city. South Carolina's newly elected governor, John Rutledge, with about 600 militia, also joined the race to defend the capital. When the portly Lincoln became aware of the British maneuver, he too puffed back up the Savannah Road to the rescue. "Never was the country in greater general confusion, consternation and alarm," a contemporary observed.

In early May troops under Moultrie and Rutledge marched into Charles Town and began preparing for Prevost's attack. Mrs. Ann Manigault observed "great uneasiness on account of the British troops"; on May 9 she entered in her diary: "Great confusion as they were very near"; two days later Mrs. Manigault wrote: "Much firing and it was expected the town would be attacked." On that same day, the Patriot and Baptist minister Oliver Hart noted that "everybody expected (and many wished) the attack would be made." He was well aware of the strong Loyalist sentiment in the town.

As General Prevost neared the outskirts of Charles Town, Loyalists, leading merchants, and planters within, concerned for their lives and property, urged Governor Rutledge to seek a compromise with the British. Although Christopher Gadsden, General Moultrie, and Colonel John Laurens vigorously argued against such a proposal, a message was sped to the British commander on May 11 stating that if the town were spared, South Carolina officials would insure the state's neutrality for the duration of the war. Prevost initially spurned the offer and pressed for unconditional surrender. But this was quickly rejected when word reached the garrison that General Lincoln and his 4,000 troops were nearing the town.

When the British forces began a withdrawal, civilian authorities within the town, still reluctant to coordinate plans with the military, sent out a small force under Major Benjamin Huger to harass Prevost. Because Moultrie's sentinels were not alerted to the mission, the force was fired on when it attempted to return to town. Huger and several of his men were killed. One resident observed that the shots fired at Huger's party were interpreted as a signal that the British were attacking and "the lines were in an instant all on a Blaze. The Roar of the cannon and small arms was comparable to terrible thunder."

On May 12 Mrs. Manigault wrote in her diary that the British had "marched off in the night"; the following day she gave a sigh of relief, "Pretty quiet." But on May 16 she wrote: "We are still very uneasy, they are ravaging the country."

After Prevost's force escaped from Lincoln's army across Wappoo Creek to James Island and headed south toward Savannah, British marauders devastated the countryside. Ashley Hall plantation was looted. The owner reported that his rum and wine cellar was pillaged and the "Library scattered and mostly carried away." A resident of Goose Creek asserted that a British scouting party "plundered" his home and "took everything they fancied & carried away all my Horses & 3 negro Boys." The Pinckney family also suffered severe financial losses. At his plantation on the Ashepoo, the newly promoted Major Thomas Pinckney discovered that the British carried off 19 Negroes, "took all the best horses, burnt the dwelling house and books, destroyed all the furniture, china, etc. killed the sheep and poultry, and drank the liquors." At his mother's home, Belmont, raiders smashed everything inside the house.

General Lincoln and his militia were unable to prevent the general "ravaging" of the nearby countryside. But the Reverend Oliver Hart asserted that General Lincoln had saved "Sinful Charles Town." Citizens of the town celebrated, but "the joyous respite was of short duration." The third British strike at the Carolina lowcountry would have a different ending.

With Prevost marching away to the south, Carolinians breathed more easily during the summer of 1779. But General Lincoln did not. From June to September he labored to keep his troops at or near Charles Town supplied with food and clothing. He pressed Congress for funds. When units among the militia forces threatened "to march off & go home" and sometimes did, he sent recruiters scurrying into the countryside to find replacements. Usually they returned emptyhanded. Finding the South Carolina militia "very inferior" soldiers anyway, he pleaded with General Washington to send him Continental troops. Lincoln warned his commander-in-chief that without reinforcements "I tremble for this State, as there will be a great danger of its being lost."

In September, 1779, still anxious to take the offensive, General Lincoln coordinated a plan of attack on Savannah with French naval and land forces under Admiral Charles-Hector, Comte d'Estaing. South Carolina military and civilian officials enthusiastically rallied to the plan. They reasoned that if the British had their hands full with an attacking force at Savannah, they would keep their hands off Charles Town.

The Franco-American campaign became a disaster. Procrastination by Admiral d'Estaing and General Lincoln, disagreements between the land and sea commanders, General Prevost's excellent defensive works, and a poorly executed assault launched on the morning of October 9 all spelled doom for the allied attackers. Nearly 300 of Lincoln's assault force were killed and hundreds of others wounded; both the "gallant Pole," Count Casimir Pulaski, and "the hero of Sullivan's Island," Sergeant William Jasper, were mortally wounded. Shot through the chest and stomach, Jasper fell clutching one of the colors presented to the Second Regiment by Susannah Elliott three years before. Admiral d'Estaing, himself wounded twice, soon set the sails of his fleet for France. General Lincoln and his badly mauled force of several thousand militia and Continentals limped back to Charles Town.

No sooner had General Lincoln arrived back in South Carolina than General Washington informed him that the British were preparing "another and more vigorous effort to the southward." "Be prepared for the worst," Washington wrote, as the British may first "proceed against Charles Town." The intelligence reports of the commander-in-chief of the America Army were correct.

When Sir Henry Clinton in New York heard of the repulse by Prevost of the Franco-American force at Savannah and the departure of the French fleet from American waters, he was elated. "I think this is the greatest event that has happened in the whole war," he exclaimed. With the Atlantic free of French ships, the way was clear for Clinton to proceed against South Carolina.

Clinton believed that Charles Town was the key to the reduction of the state. He planned to lead the attack in person. On the cold, but bright day after Christmas, 1779, Clinton joined Vice Admiral Marriot Arbuthnot's fleet off New York; 90 transports loaded with over 8,000 troops, horses, heavy guns, and provisions supported by heavily armed fighting ships slipped their anchors and steered southward before "a fair wind." From the deck of the man-of-war *Romulus* General Sir Henry Clinton mused: "This is the most important hour Britain ever knew."

At Charles Town General Lincoln was still beleaguered by the problems of constructing adequate defensive works, and of finding adequate clothing, food, arms, ammunition, and sufficient numbers of troops. An epidemic of smallpox which swept across the lowcountry in the fall further complicated his problems. Appeals

Courtesy South Carolina Historical Society

Vice Admiral Marriott Arbuthnot

by Governor Rutledge to the backcountry militia to march to Charles Town's defense fell on deaf ears when the cry of "pox" went up along the coast. Slaves constructing defensive works about the town were felled by the disease, and the remaining healthy ones had to be evacuated before they became infected.

But in December, Lincoln was heartened. His urgent pleas to Congress and General Washington for troops and supplies were partially met. On December 22 a supply ship with "military stores" from Philadelphia entered the Charles Town harbor. The following day South Carolina's senior sea captain and Continental commodore, Abram Whipple, arrived off the bar with four armed frigates. Lincoln also learned that 750 Continental troops under Brigadier General William Woodford were quickstepping toward the town. And when the smallpox epidemic ran its course in late December, construction on the defensive works about the town resumed.

Believing that Fort Moultrie on Sullivan's Island, batteries at Haddrell's Point, Fort Johnson on James Island, Commodore Whipple's squadron, and the natural defensive bar across the harbor mouth would prevent a British assault from the sea, General Lincoln assumed that any attack would have to come from the northwestern or land side of Charles Town. Acting on this assumption, he decided to wall up his force within the peninsula town.

Courtesy Carolina Art Association/Gibbes Museum of Art

Encampment at Haddrell's Point Near Present-day Mount Pleasant
(from 1776-1780 batteries were located here to
protect Charles Town from an assault from the sea)

Just to the north of Boundary Street, Calhoun Street today, Lincoln ordered the building of a series of redoubts and trenches linking the Ashley and Cooper Rivers. At the same time he ordered the felling of trees and the leveling of a few houses on the peninsula neck in order to remove possible "cover to the enemy in case of a siege." However, citizens of the town who owned the property objected strenuously. Several were influential advisors to Governor Rutledge. Once again the military commander of the town faced political pressure from the civilian officials; once again the Patriot cause was subordinated to powerful propertied interests. Only under pressure from Governor Rutledge was a compromise reached. A portion of the woods was cut down and a few houses demolished.

By early 1780, Lincoln's breastworks were nearing completion. A line of trenches, batteries, and oyster shell and mortar redoubts linked the swamps and rivers lying to the east and west of the peninsula. Just to the front of the works a network of abatis—sharpened stakes embedded at an angle — was implanted. Beyond these, "at ye distance of a musquet shot," Lincoln told General Washington, engineers and gangs of slaves excavated a ditch 6 feet deep and 12 feet wide. The batteries at Fort Moultrie, commanded by Colonel Charles Cotesworth Pinckney, and those at Fort Johnson were primed and manned. Commodore Whipple's four frigates and several barges were stationed in the channel off Fort Moultrie. Lincoln now believed that "we should not be easily insulted" by the British so long as Charles Town was manned by "a proper garrison." Adequate troop strength and well-disciplined soldiers remained his major worry.

Lincoln was constantly bothered by the number of men he observed "strolling about the streets" when they were supposed to be on duty; he agonized over the "alarming consequences" when he found men sleeping on sentinel duty; and he continued to doubt the usefulness of the South Carolina militia "until all of them are really influenced by those principles of Patriotism, that love of their Country, and concern for their own freedom and independence, [necessary] to oppose the tyranny of Britain." It was such concern which prompted him to ask the South Carolina Assembly to authorize the arming of Negro slaves.

This proposal followed close on the heels of a recommendation by the Continental Congress supported by Henry Laurens that slaves be enlisted, armed, clothed, and fed "at the expense of the United States." Owners of the slave enlistees would receive full compensation up to $1,000. If the enlistees served faithfully and survived, they were to be emancipated at the end of the war.

As the Assembly had refused such a request by General Lincoln in 1779, so too did the legislative body refuse his request in early 1780. Facing imminent attack and the possible reduction of Charles Town, the lowcountry aristocracy tenaciously resisted any tampering with the very foundations of their economic and social life. Obviously at the very highest cost they planned to protect the institution of slavery. Fear of insurrections by the armed slaves was also an equally important factor for the Assembly in rejecting Lincoln's request. Christopher Gadsden best summarized the feeling of the lowcountry elite when he declared: "We are much disgusted at recommending us to arm our slaves; it was received with great resentment as a very dangerous and impolitic step."

Only with great reluctance did the Legislature eventually sanction the enlisting of 1,000 slaves as unarmed oarsmen and general laborers. A few slaves were used as spies. In an unusual case the lowcountry slave Antigua and his family were granted their freedom by the South Carolina Legislature for gaining intelligence within British lines at great personal risk.

"Under apprehension of the British," Mrs. Ann Manigault wrote into her diary on the evening of January 22, 1780. Several nights later she confided: "We are much afraid. People go out of town very fast." The news was sweeping across the lowcountry — "a number of transports, store ships, and other vessels to the amount of about ninety" were off North Edisto Inlet.

Sir Henry Clinton's anticipated two-week voyage from New York waters to battle stations off Carolina's coast had been stretched to nearly seven weeks by "perverse winds" and mountainous, rolling seas. Clinton described the trip down the coast as "a dreadful voyage with loss of almost everything, baggage, horses, etc." But by February 14 Admiral Arbuthnot had moved his fleet into the North Edisto River, and General Clinton was directing the disembarkation of 6,000 troops at Simmons (now Seabrook) Island just 20-odd miles to the south of Charles Town. He waited until the end of February for reinforcements and supplies, and then marched his well-equipped army of nearly 10,000 strong north toward the South Carolina capital.

From the steeple of St. Michael's, the highest vantage point in Charles Town, Patriot editor Peter Timothy with spyglass to eye saw the smoke rise from a thousand British campfires as the troops moved from sea island to sea island up the coast. Southeast to seaward he saw the first ships of their fleet paralleling the line of march. Throughout February and March he passed his observations along to General Lincoln.

The commander at Charles Town now realized that he faced a "very critical situation of having troops shut up

Courtesy South Carolina Historical Society

Charles Town, 1780
(from St. Michael's Steeple on the left Peter Timothy
watched the British fleet approach)

in a besieged town." But in mid-February, Lincoln told
Governor Rutledge that "no consideration could induce
me to adopt a new mode of conduct or would justify my
doing it." In turn, Rutledge reassured Lincoln of full
cooperation from all South Carolinians who had such
an important stake in defending the capital of the state.
A few weeks later Lincoln was shocked to learn that a
South Carolina Continental officer, Colonel Hamilton
Ballendine, was planning to supply the British with
information concerning the town's defensive works.
Colonel Ballendine was apprehended, and Lincoln's
justice was swift. He ordered the spy hanged.

By late February Clinton and his troops had moved from
John's Island to James Island. "The people are much
distressed," Ann Manigault wrote. In early March the
British seized Fort Johnson. They now commanded the
southern approach to the harbor and controlled the entire west bank of the Ashley River.

General Clinton had decided on his plan of attack. He
would march his army around the harbor defenses,

cross the Ashley to the peninsula neck, and establish siege lines facing the American works. At the same time Admiral Arbuthnot would secure control of the harbor and rivers. If this classic siege plan of encirclement by land and sea succeeded, it would prevent any attempts at reinforcement or escape. Charles Town and its defenders would be doomed.

Hope surged through the defenders of Charles Town on March 3. Brigadier General James Hogun marched into the city with 700 North Carolina Continentals and caused "great happiness and spirit," Lincoln informed General Washington.

In early March, Lincoln redoubled his efforts to improve the defenses of the town. Realizing that Commodore Whipple's frigates and barges were no match for the heavily armed British warships gathering off the harbor bar, Lincoln ordered Whipple to move into the Cooper River and obstruct it. Eleven vessels, including the four Continental frigates, were scuttled near the mouth of the Cooper, and a boom was strung to connect the masts of the submerged hulls. To guard his last remaining route of escape from the city, Lincoln sent General Isaac Huger and 500 cavalry to Monck's Corner about 30 miles to the northwest.

Commodore Whipple, after sinking his ships in the Cooper's mouth, offered his talents for the defense of the town. Believing that St. Michael's Church steeple would provide the gunners on British vessels an excellent aiming point, Whipple ordered the seaward side of the steeple painted black. By this the commodore hoped to "render it less distinct." But to his chagrin the steeple now stood out more distinctly than before. Ever after citizens of the town referred to him as "cunning Commodore Whipple."

Until late March, the harbor's natural defenses caused Admiral Arbuthnot and General Clinton more trouble than the American defenders. The admiral experienced great difficulties in getting his ships across the bar; therefore, the general, in need of sailors and small craft to ferry his troops over the Ashley River to the peninsula neck, could only wait on the west bank. Not until March 20 did the English ships cross into the harbor. "Joy to you, Sir, to myself, and to us all upon your passage of that infernal bar," Clinton exclaimed to one of the fleet officers.

Now with small boats provided by the fleet, Clinton rapidly moved his troops across the Ashley unopposed. By April 3 his engineers had constructed a line of trenches and redoubts two miles in length connecting the Ashley and Cooper Rivers and running parallel and just 800 yards from the defensive works of Charles Town. Digging and entrenching as they went, Clinton's troops inched their complex forward during early April. Batteries on both sides began exchanging cannonades. Two Hessian officers serving with the British force noted that April 5 was a day of incessant cannonading. Staff Captain Johann Hinrich observed that "the enemy fired over seven hundred shots." Returning the fire, British batteries sent crossbar shot into the town which "made a terrific clatter on the houses," Captain Johann Ewald remembered. Both officers heard shouts and screams from within the American defenses. Captain Hinrich thought they sounded like " 'Oh, murder! Oh, Lord!' "

A siege mentality gripped the city. After nightfall guards posted atop St. Michael's Church were to sound "all's well" and ring the bells every 15 minutes; sentinels throughout the town were ordered to take up the cry. At dawn each day a patrol was sent just beyond the

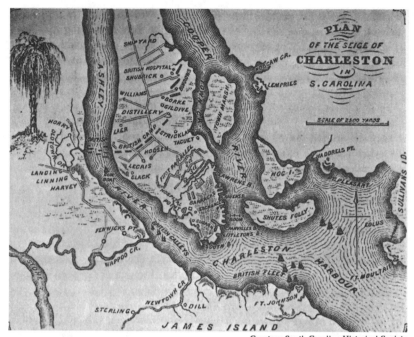

Courtesy South Carolina Historical Society

Plan of the Siege of Charles Town, 1780

lines to insure that the British had not crept up to the outer works under cover of darkness. To sound the alarm for a general attack on the lines, three cannons at the horn work or main redoubt were to be fired at two-minute intervals.

On the morning of April 7, General Clinton was informed that "the rebels sent off many of their women." In the afternoon the defenders enjoyed one of their last leaps of hope. The long-awaited 750 North Carolina Continentals under General William Woodford marched in. A captain in the British force heard the defenders cheer so loudly, ring bells so long, and fire so many salvos from their cannons and muskets that he and other officers ran for their arms. "None of us doubted but that the enemy had made a sortie," he wrote. They soon learned, however, that the defenders were merely celebrating Woodford's arrival. Now Lincoln commanded over 5,000 Continentals and militiamen within the city.

The buoyed hopes of the day before blew away on April 8. Taking advantage of a strong southeast breeze and a flood tide, Admiral Arbuthnot sent eight ships dashing downchannel past Fort Moultrie. Colonel Pinckney's gunners unloosed a furious barrage, but inflicted only superficial damage on the fast-flying frigates. They anchored off James Island within broadside range of the town. Fort Moultrie had been neutralized as a point of defense.

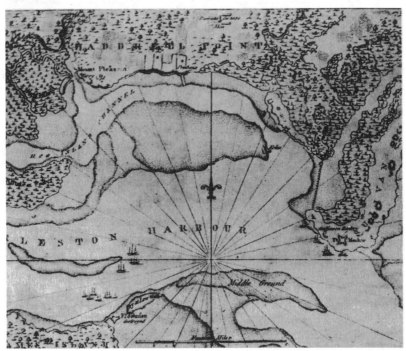

Courtesy South Carolina Historical Society

A Sketch of the Charles Town Harbor Showing the Disposition of the British Fleet, 1780

On the morning of April 10, Charles Town defenders observed several officers from the British Army approaching the lines under a flag of truce. They brought a message from Clinton and Arbuthnot demanding that Lincoln either surrender "the Town and Garrison" or risk "Havoc and Desolation." General Lincoln quickly sent a message back to the British officers informing them that he planned to defend Charles Town "to the last extremity."

During the next several days the British brought heavy artillery closer to the town. Officers of the fleet and a few under Clinton hoped to set the town ablaze and quickly end the siege. They joked about sending some "twenty-four pound shot into the stomachs of the women to see how they will deliver them."

On the morning of April 13, the British big guns opened a bombardment of the town with round shot and incendiary bombs. A French officer within observed that "the fire was very vigorous and we replied to it with all the artillery in town." British shells bursting about the works and inside damaged the defenses, set houses afire, and killed or wounded several townspeople and soldiers. Clinton was incensed. He ordered an immediate halt to the effort to burn the town and damned as "absurd, impolitic, and inhuman" any attempt "to burn a town you mean to occupy."

On the same day of the bombardment Lincoln began re-evaluating his position. Plagued by shortages of "provisions, stores and artillery," and advised by his engineers that the "fortifications could hold out but a few days more," he summoned his officers to consider an evacuation of the town. They only resolved, however, that Governor Rutledge and several advisors should depart immediately. This they did, leaving Lieutenant Governor Christopher Gadsden as the ranking civilian official among the besieged.

The day following Governor Rutledge's flight, any option for evacuating the American Army at Charles Town was closed. Striking suddenly before dawn on April 14, Colonel Banastre Tarleton, leading a combined force of British dragoons and Loyalists, shot-up and scattered General Huger's cavalry at Monck's Corner. Now all territory east of the Cooper River fell to the British. Lincoln was left with no avenue of escape. Clinton's encirclement of Charles Town was complete.

The British forces inched their lines closer to the city's defenses. An officer inside the town wrote on April 15: "The enemy made a constant musket fire on our lines"; two days later he recorded: "There was a very brisk mortar and howitzer fire which wounded about thirty of our men." On the same day the Hessian Captain Johann Ewald observed: "The enemy fired upon our workmen all night with small arms and grapeshot, wounding five grenadiers."

By April 19, the redcoats were within 250 yards of the American lines. That same day General Lincoln called a meeting of his officers and the civilian officials to consider capitulation. A majority of his generals supported him, but the usually abrasive and hot-tempered Lieutenant Governor Gadsden became abusive. He damned any "thought of capitulation." Colonel Charles Cotesworth Pinckney stood with Gadsden and denounced his fellow officers. He called them defeatists. A civilian official warned Lincoln that if he attempted "to carry off the Continental troops," the citizens would "open the gates for the enemy" before Lincoln could evacuate the city.

Despite such demands to hold the town at any price, Lincoln, knowing his situation to be desperate, sent surrender terms to Clinton on April 21. Among his stipulations was the provision for the peaceful withdrawal of the American troops, their arms, and provisions. Clinton promptly and curtly refused such terms.

By late April the British had drained the canal before the American lines, crossed over it, and were entrenching and constructing redoubts at the edge of the abatis. They were so close that pistol and musket fire could be brought to rake the streets of the town.

In a desperation move, an American force of 150 men made a lightning sortie against the nearest English re-

The Siege of Charles Town from the British Lines, 1780

doubt at daybreak on April 24. Surprising the British, they killed or wounded about a dozen troops in a brief firefight, took others prisoner, and raced back to their own lines. When Clinton heard of the raid he believed his troops had been caught "a little off guard."

The attack by the Americans was an aberration. The British pressed forward relentlessly. Within the garrisoned town food supplies were running out. One defender wrote: "Our rations of meat reduced to six ounces; coffee and sugar allowed only to the soldiers."

Knowing that the Americans were running low on food, the British, tradition has it, fired a non-combustible shell into town containing molasses and rice. Perhaps it was an early attempt at psychological warfare. The defenders, however, returned the gesture by charging the same shell with sulphur and hog's fat and fired it back into the British lines so that they might use it to combat the itch.

Their artillery ammunition also nearly spent, the defenders could not halt the British advance. Captain Peter Russell, an officer in Clinton's force, noticed that the Americans had been reduced to firing "ragged pieces of Iron, broken bottles etc, old axes, gun barrels, tomawhawks etc."

On May 7 Admiral Arbuthnot landed an attack force of British seamen on Sullivan's Island. They took Fort Moultrie without resistance. Defenders within Charles Town that same day were astonished to see the English flag flying over the fort. They wondered how the embattlement "had been taken since the night had been quiet."

When word leaked out in early May that General Clinton was readying his forces for a general assault on the town, several American ladies went to see him. They desired, Clinton wrote, "I should permit them to go into town to take leave of their sons." Graciously he granted their wishes. "Tout est permis aux dames," Clinton said.

Before launching his full-scaled assault, Clinton attempted to make a last effort to negotiate surrender terms with the besieged. His conditions were the same as before, and he urged General Lincoln to stop "persevering in a fruitless Defense."

There was nearly unanimous agreement among the military officers under Lincoln's command and civilians in the town to accept the terms. Only two highly vocal men still had strong reservations, Colonel Charles Cotesworth Pinckney and Lieutenant Governor Christopher Gadsden. For reasons of both honor and military necessity Pinckney called for resistance to the end. The British would be badly mauled if they attacked the town, Pinckney argued, although many Americans too might die. But to make death "useful to one's country," he believed, was "the greatest felicity a patriotic soldier can hope for." Although by now the fiery Gadsden accepted surrender as inevitable, he urged Lincoln to seek terms which would permit Patriots time to set their personal effects in order and to leave the state. This Lincoln proposed to Clinton. It was the main reason that the British general rejected the conditional surrender terms proposed by the Americans. Now General Clinton resolved "to bring this business to a quick decision." He ordered a bombardment of the town to begin on the evening of May 9.

Throughout the night and into the next day and the next, a defender wrote, "musket fire, grape-shot, bombs, and red-hot cannon balls" from 200 British guns crashed and exploded about the works and town. Sporadically the defenders returned the cannonading.

But within the town the "fire was really dreadful and within our lines did great execution," an American observed. Twenty houses were hit and set afire. Bucket brigades of slaves raced from one conflagration to another. General Moultrie observed that the British bombardment "was incessant, cannon balls whizzing and shells hissing continually amongst us; ammunition chests and temporary magazines blowing up; great guns bursting and wounded men groaning along the lines." At night the defenders saw mortar shells "bursting in the air" and crisscrossing in the sky "like meteors. It appeared as if the stars were tumbling down." Exploding shells "wretchedly mangled" some defenders.

On the afternoon of May 11 as British troops prepared for an assault on the town, a Hessian officer serving with Clinton watched "the enemy hoist a large white flag." At long last the Americans were capitulating. The ferocious bombardment had convinced even the most diehard defender that further resistance was futile, foolish, or both. Even Christopher Gadsden enjoined Lincoln to accept whatever surrender terms were offered.

Arrangements were quickly worked out between the contending commanders. About mid-afternoon on May 12, a British officer saw "Lincoln limping out [of the town] at the head of the most ragged rabble I ever beheld." Their colors cased, their drums beating a Turkish march, the defenders stacked arms before their works. A French officer among the Americans wrote that "at half after three a company of English Grenadiers and another of Hessians took possession." General Lincoln received Major General Alexander Leslie at the gate and officially surrendered the town. More British troops filed past the defenders and to the accompaniment of oboists blowing "God Save the King," they raised the royal standard over the town gate and fired off a 22-gun salute. Some

South Carolinians shared the lament of the Reverend Oliver Hart: "Often, often did I wrestle with God with fervent prayers and tears, that poor Charles Town might be spared, and not suffered to fall into the enemy's hands. Never could I give it up, until I heard of its surrender."

General Lincoln surrendered an army of nearly 5,500 men, their weapons, ammunition, and stores; he turned over to the British the last open-sea port, seven generals, and the second highest official in the state government, Lieutenant Governor Christopher Gadsden. The fight was over for the only army in the Southern theatre of the war. Lincoln and his Continentals became prisoners. The officers were confined in barracks near present-day Mount Pleasant, but allowed liberal privileges. Colonel Charles Cotesworth Pinckney, for instance, was permitted to keep a black body slave who ran errands for him. Pinckney's family and friends were allowed to visit. The enlisted regular troops became prisoners of war on British transports in the harbor. Most would be exchanged within a year. Initially, South Carolina militia and civilians were treated as prisoners on parole.

As General Sir Henry Clinton had hoped upon departure from New York the year before, the capture of Charles Town was one of England's finest hours. It would be the greatest victory of the war for the English; it would be America's greatest defeat of the entire war.

When word of the capitulation of Charles Town spread to Loyalists in America and to Englishmen abroad, toasts were drunk and celebrations begun. In London's Hyde Park several thousand British regulars were drawn up to fire off salvos from muskets and cannons; Parliament congratulated the general and the admiral on their great victory. American Loyalists greeted them as conquering heroes.

CHAPTER IV

The British Occupation

General Clinton's estimate that the key to Carolina's collapse would be Charles Town's capture proved correct. Within a few months, the British controlled all of South Carolina, and Loyalists were streaming to the King's colors. Many came to Charles Town; many were already there.

Clinton established his headquarters in the Miles Brewton House on lower Meeting Street, one of the town's most magnificent homes. The mistress of the house, Mrs. Rebecca Brewton Motte, kept her three young daughters confined to the attic lest the British officers and men hurrying in and out act unlike gentlemen.

From this headquarters Clinton launched a policy aimed at the political reconciliation of South Carolinians to the crown. In late May, the British commander issued a proclamation to the citizens promising them pardon of all "treasonable offenses" if they renounced their parole and took an oath of allegiance to the British government. Clinton had been advised that there were "people of the first fortunes" in Charles Town who realized their "errors" and were ready to reaffirm their loyalties. He was not disappointed.

The proclamation produced the "most happy effects"; many inhabitants came to headquarters bringing "their former oppressors," Clinton wrote. One hundred and ten of the "principal and most respectable inhabitants of Charles Town" addressed a memorial to the British commander on June 3, 1780. They pledged their loyalty to England and tendered to Clinton their "warmest congratulations on the Restoration of this Capitol and Province to their political connection with the Crown and Government of Great Britain." Some nimblefooted businessmen, ardent Patriots when the Americans were in control, now seeing potentially fat profits on wartime trade, were leaping to become equally ardent Loyalists now that the British were in control.

Mrs. Rebecca Brewton Motte

Among the once prominent Patriots of the lowcountry who abruptly shifted their loyalties were Henry Middleton and Charles Pinckney. Middleton had been President of the First Continental Congress; Pinckney had been the former President of the South Carolina Legislature. Both now pledged their allegiance to the crown. The aged Gabriel Manigault who had loaned more money to the American cause than any other man in South Carolina shifted his loyalties. So, too, did his grandson, Gabriel Manigault, Jr. Daniel Cannon, influential artisan and cohort of Gadsden, took the oath, pledging himself to be "a true and faithful subject to His Majesty the King of Great Britain." Daniel Huger, an aide to Governor Rutledge, exchanged his parole status for a pardon and took the oath of loyalty. So, too, did Colonel Isaac Hayne and dozens of the less prominent.

Sir Henry Clinton might have succeeded in making the town "an asylum for the friends of the government" had he not appointed Lieutenant Colonel Nisbet Balfour the commandant of Charles Town. Some citizens soon became contemptuous of this fighting soldier who had distinguished himself at Bunker Hill and New York. To them Balfour had "all the frivolous self-importance, and all the disgusting insolence, which are natural to little minds when puffed up by their sudden elevation, and employed in functions to which their abilities are not equal." General Moultrie, after several encounters with Balfour, characterized him as a "proud, haughty Scot" of a "tyrannical insolent disposition." He "treated the people as the most abject slaves." Balfour's administration proved to be of more help to the American cause than to the British.

Surrounded by redcoated soldiers and Loyalist civilians and ruled over by Balfour, a few militant Patriots managed to keep the American cause at Charles Town barely alive. About 30 prominent civilians refused to take the oath of loyalty to the crown and by their "silent example" probably influenced others to follow suit.

Overall responsibility for the town and the British department of the South fell on the shoulders of Major General Charles, Lord Cornwallis after Clinton's departure for New York. By the late summer of 1780, Cornwallis was concerned about that group of men in the town who had been the "Ring-leaders of Rebellion" in South Carolina. Cornwallis and Balfour discovered that they not only refused to take the oath, but were holding "constant meetings from which they carried on a correspondence with the enemy." Encouraged themselves by the news of partisan Patriot bands operating in the countryside, these few Patriot citizens of Charles Town were succoring other Patriot-leaning townspeople and bullying Loyalists. Cornwallis decided that they could not be allowed to remain in Charles Town and ordered Balfour to remove them.

Colonel Balfour decided to ship the "ringleaders" to St. Augustine, British East Florida. To justify his actions, he announced that a plot had been uncovered to burn the town and to massacre the loyal subjects. During the night of August 28 British soldiers knocked on the doors of those suspected of "seditious activities" and arrested them. They were then herded aboard the ship *Sandwich* in the harbor. Outraged, they protested being treated as common felons and objected to "the severe manner in which we were taken up and the scandalous method made use of in conveying us from our habitations." In no way, they declared, had they violated their paroles. As might be expected, Christopher Gadsden, among those arrested, made it known to British officials that he was the most outraged of all.

But the Patriots' protests were to no avail. Balfour told them that for "reasons of [British] policy it was necessary that the place of their residence be changed," and the *Sandwich* soon set sail for St. Augustine. Besides Gadsden, those aboard included Edward Rutledge; Alexander Moultrie, brother of General Moultrie; Thomas Heyward, Jr., signer of the Declaration of Independence; Peter Timothy, editor of the *Gazette*; and Dr. David Ramsay, later one of South Carolina's foremost historians. About a year later some of these men were allowed to join their families in Philadelphia where they had been banished.

Courtesy Independence National Historical Park Collection, Philadelphia

Thomas Heyward, Jr.
(exiled from Charles Town by the British in 1780)

The exile of these "ringleaders" did not end clandestine operations against the British at Charles Town. Colonel Balfour was particularly attentive to ferreting out smuggling rings which he believed operated within the town. Throughout 1780 and 1781 he fretted over the boots, saddlery, arms, and intelligence flowing from "rebels" in town to partisan backcountry bands.

Thomas Singleton's home on Church Street was often the site of midnight meetings between Patriots who slipped in and out of town seeking money and information to carry out partisan activities. When the British occasionally apprehended suspects for sending intelligence beyond the town, they were confined in the "damp, unwholesome" basement of the Exchange Building. These political prisoners were incarcerated with common criminals of both sexes. As the Exchange basement filled up, ships in the harbor were converted to floating jails for suspects and for those who continued to refuse to take the oath of loyalty. Some Patriots later claimed that prisoners in the Exchange and aboard the ships contracted dysentery and "jail fever." They witnessed "much sickness and some deaths." But reports were inconsistent. When Mrs. Eliza Wilkinson visited the British prison ships in the summer of 1781, she "drank coffee with the prisoners [and found] the dear fellows in high spirits."

Believing that he had failed to interdict the flow of supplies and intelligence from Charles Town to the backcountry, and angry at those who persisted in refusing to take the loyalty oath, Balfour sanctioned economic reprisals. Policies established by the Board of Police, a powerful body created by the British to govern the town during the occupation, served to legalize the reprisals. For instance, "rebels" were not allowed to appear before the Board to bring suit against debtors, but

Loyalists could summon "rebels" to answer similar charges. By 1781, the Board prohibited those not taking the oath from engaging in business. This moved some merchants and artisans to become "loyal" subjects in order to survive. A few fled the town to join partisan bands.

By May, 1781, crown officials of Charles Town viewed all citizens who had not professed their loyalty as "Inveterate Enemies of the British Government." The policies of the Board and Balfour were pushing some citizens from the position of "silent" protestors into that of actively supporting the Patriot partisans.

An incident in August, 1781, particularly embittered Patriot residents of the town. Colonel Isaac Hayne, who had taken the pledge of allegiance to the King on the fall of Charles Town, soon broke his oath and took up arms again. In July, 1781, he was captured by the British while leading a raid near the town. Colonel Balfour and other British officials in South Carolina already were irritated by the wholesale numbers of men who had first professed loyalty to King then taken up arms against him. Additionally, they were aware of the numerous atrocities that had been committed against Loyalists throughout the backcountry. Such cases prompted Colonel Balfour to write from Charles Town in May, 1781: "Many have been the outrages committed by the American troops, and their violations of all the humaner principles of war." Balfour was concerned especially with reports of "the rigorous treatment, in many cases extending unto death, which the Loyal Militia when made prisoners, most invariable experience." A ruthless civil war was raging across the Southern backcountry between wandering and marauding bands of Loyalists and Patriots.

Perhaps Balfour had heard of such men as Captain Patrick "Paddy" Carr who committed numerous atrocities against Loyalist civilians and militia alike. It was known at the time that Carr never gave quarter to Loyalists as "prisoners, or as enemies in battle. He hunted them down like wild beasts" and executed them. It appears that some British officers in South Carolina believed that Colonel Isaac Hayne himself had led an attack on a hospital convoy of redcoats and committed "extraordinary acts of brutality" on the sick and wounded.

These considerations, and the need of an extreme example to show that they meant business, prompted Balfour and Lieutenant Colonel Francis, Lord Rawdon, now supreme commander in South Carolina, jointly to issue orders for Hayne's execution. On August 4, 1781, he was hanged in Charles Town. Many mourned his death, but by making an example of him the British prompted some who had taken up arms after taking the oath of loyalty to lay them down again. About a month after Hayne's execution, Governor John Rutledge, whose rolling carriage was the seat of the Patriot government of South Carolina, wrote: "The execution of Hayne had the effect which the enemy foresaw." But the British at Charles Town could not stamp out the less overt and more subtle evidences of hostility to their presence which persisted among a few citizens.

The same Thomas Singleton who opened his home on Church Street to midnight "rebel" gatherings, despised the British officer class. Balfour was especially distasteful to him. To demonstrate his contempt, Singleton dressed a pet baboon in a scaled-down but exact replica of the commandant's uniform and addressed the animal as Colonel Balfour.

By verbal assaults, outspoken support of their husbands' cause and even a few clandestine acts, the Patriot
ladies of Charles Town harassed the British garrison.

When Mr. Isaac Holmes was aroused in the early hours
of August 28, 1780, and arrested as a "rebel ringleader,"
Mrs. Holmes accompanied him out of the house. To the
irritation of the arresting British soldiers, she shouted
out to her husband: "Waver not in your principles, but
be true to your country." Soon after Mrs. Charles Elliott
heard that her father, Thomas Ferguson, had been arrested and confined on the *Sandwich* soon to depart for
St. Augustine, she gained permission to go aboard to bid
him goodbye. Accompanied by the captain of the ship
she met with her father. In an effort to soothe emotions
during the tearful reunion and to be hospitable, the
British captain asked if they would like a *French*
liqueur. In response, a contemporary later recalled, Mrs.
Elliott cried out, "God bless the nation." Turning to her
father she implored him not to let the present "oppres-
sion shake your fortitude nor cause you to swerve from
your duty. The valour of your countrymen, aided by
friendly France, will speedily dissipate the gloom of our
immediate prospects."

Some months later as Mrs. Elliott strolled in a Charles
Town garden, a passing British officer asked the name
of the flourishing camellias in the garden. Why that is
"the Rebel Flower," Mrs. Elliott reportedly told him.
According to tradition, he then inquired as to the origin
of the name and she snapped, "Because it *thrives most*
when most *trampled upon.*"

Although Mrs. Elliott persistently but subtly an-
tagonized the British officers, a friend believed that she
also "rendered them the slaves of her will." With her
"natural ease of manners, great cheerfullness in conversation, and a captivating sportivness of disposition,"

she often conned the British garrison out of certain luxuries and then sent them along to Patriot soldiers in the field. At the same time she continued to visit among the Patriots of the town reviving and sustaining "hope and inspiring a confidence of success" for American arms.

Following the Battle of Guilford Court House, North Carolina, in March, 1781, where a British army won the field from General Nathanael Greene, Charles Town inhabitants were instructed to illuminate their windows with candles to celebrate the victory. When the home of Mrs. Thomas Heyward remained shrouded in darkness, a British officer went to investigate. At the appearance of Mrs. Heyward, whose husband had been exiled to St. Augustine, the officer demanded an explanation for failure to illuminate the house. She replied, tradition has it, that since her husband was confined as a political prisoner she could feel no "spark of joy" at a British victory. The officer rejoined that her personal problems were of no consequence and commanded Mrs. Heyward to put candles in her windows. Haughty, proud, and as contemptuous of British officialdom as some lowcountry elite had long been, she replied, "not a single light shall be placed with my consent, on such an occasion." The officer then threatened to raise a force to raze her house. But refusing to be bullied, Mrs. Heyward emphatically reiterated, *"I will not illuminate."*

Several months later on the anniversary of the successful conclusion of the British siege of Charles Town, May 12, 1781, another illumination was ordered. Again Mrs. Heyward refused to comply. This time a mob of Loyalists gathered and angrily assailed her house "with brickbats, and every species of nauseating trash that could offend or annoy." A day or two later when British authorities apologized for the mob violence and offered to repair the damages, Mrs. Heyward thanked them but

"The Swamp Fox" Crosses the Pee Dee River

refused the gesture. She believed that British officials should have prevented the incident in the first place. She desired that the damages remain unrepaired, mute testimony to official inaction and the "insults" done her home.

In early 1782, as General Nathanael Greene's army moved closer to Charles Town and began to threaten the British garrison itself, a Mrs. Brewton came to town to visit relatives. Shortly after she arrived, a British officer inquired as to "the news in the country." She quickly replied "that all nature smiled, for everything was *Greene* down to Monck's Corner."

Despite such *bons mots*, the British continued to tolerate Mrs. Brewton, for awhile anyway. Some officers, attracted by her vivacious personality and intelligence, even sought her company. When one officer was assigned to a patrol beyond the town, he asked Mrs. Brewton if he might carry any of her personal letters to friends in the countryside. "No," she replied, "I should like to write, but have no idea of having my letters read at the head of Marion's Brigade." Prophetically, a few days later the same British officer on reconnaissance duty near Charles Town was captured by troops under "The Swamp Fox."

Later in the same year as Mrs. Brewton was walking down Broad Street shrouded in a black mourning dress which Patriot ladies often wore while the British occupied Charles Town, an English officer joined her. When "a crepe flounce was accidentally torn from her dress," a resident remembered years later, she picked it up, and passing the former home of Governor Rutledge, now occupied by a British colonel, she stopped. In the presence of her escort she tied the black strip of cloth to the railing while crying out, "where are you dearest Governor. I cause your house as well as your friends to mourn your absence." The catalog of Mrs. Brewton's snide and insulting remarks and her patriotic gestures—some perhaps apocryphal—had become too numerous for the British to tolerate. Within a few hours she was arrested and was soon banished to Philadelphia for the duration of the war.

British efforts to stop the flow of supplies and military intelligence out of Charles Town to the backcountry were sometimes foiled by Patriot petticoats. One of Charles Town's Revolutionary generation, Alexander Garden, wrote: "The contrivances adopted by the ladies, to carry from the British Garrison supplies to the gallant defenders of their country, were highly creditable to their ingenuity, and of infinite utility to their friends."

Courtesy Carolina Art Association/Gibbes Museum of Art

General Francis Marion in His Swamp Encampment Inviting
a British Officer to Dine

The folds of four or five petticoats normally worn beneath outer garments furnished excellent hiding places for goods to be smuggled past inquisitive British soldiers guarding access routes from the town. Cloth for military uniforms, maps, caps, cockades, epaulettes, feathers, and sometimes large boots worn on tiny feet, yet concealed by flowing skirts, moved unseen past the vigilant sentries. Such items were "so cunningly hid," wrote the romantic Garden, that the recipient "could have been no true Knight, who did not feel the obligation *to defend them to the last extremity.*"

However, there were Charles Town women who did consort with the British officers and enlisted men. During the traditional social season from January to May, crown officials and Loyalist citizens gave lavish balls and concerts. The ladies of the town were invited to these affairs. But those who accepted the invitations were shunned by the unswerving Patriot women. One recalled that those ladies who became "too fond of the British officers" were ostracized.

Unable to find sufficient white feminine companionship, British officers sometimes sought companionship among the black women of the town. At the beginning of the social season in February, 1782, an expensive grand ball was held in one of the town's most elegantly furnished homes. Presiding over the affair were three Negro women "dressed up in the richest silks," a spectator noted. Following a several course meal costing over 80 pounds sterling, British officers and elegantly attired slave women danced away the evening.

British officers garrisoned at Charles Town pursued pleasure with a vigor. They commandeered the most elegantly furnished homes for their quarters and the "luxuries of the [wine] cellars" for their palates. They joined such Loyalist-dominated organizations as the St. Andrew's Society and the Hunt Club. Here they devoted themselves to dining and drinking. To the distaste of the Patriots remaining in the town the King's birthdays were turned into celebrations of feasting and drinking, featuring the firing of muskets and cannons, the ringing of bells, and the playing of "God Save the King" throughout the day.

Royal officials frequently were entertained in the private homes of Loyalists. Dr. George Carter, who had taken the oath of loyalty out of financial necessity so that he could continue practicing medicine to feed his family, but who remained sympathetic to the Patriot cause, often invited British officers to his home. On one occasion he entertained a few of his friends who shared his feelings and several British officers at a seated dinner. Towards the end of the evening, as the party began to break up, he glanced around the table, and, thinking that all but his close friends had left, Dr. Carter proposed a toast. Raising his glass, he shouted: "To the American Congress." As he prepared to toss off the drink, a voice from a far dark corner of the room rasped: "What is that you say? Do you mean to insult us with such a toast?" Realizing that at least one royal officer remained, Dr. Carter quickly and shrewdly responded: "My dear friend hear me out. I meant to add, 'may they all be hanged.' " The British officer, now satisfied, raised his own glass and drank down the toast.

As British officers and Loyalist civilians came to dominate the business, civil, and social life of the town, the authorities insured also that supporters of the crown controlled the churches and the schools. Crown officials removed the Patriot ministers of St. Michael's and St. Philip's and replaced them with Loyalists. The Reverend Robert Cooper, tossed out by the Patriot vestry as the minister of St. Michael's for pro-crown sentiments in 1776, returned from exile in England to become the rector of St. Philip's. Unquestioning loyalty was demanded from the schoolmasters of the town. When two teachers thought to be crown sympathizers were reported teaching their students dangerous "rebel" ideas, they were banished from Charles Town in 1781.

In the late summer of that same year, the Rhode Island-born, fighting Quaker General Nathanael Greene and his ragged Continentals fell on a British force at Eutaw Springs. During the fierce battle by the banks of the slow-moving Santee about 50 miles from Charles Town, the British sustained heavy losses. They were forced to withdraw to Charles Town. It was the last major British force operating in the field in Georgia and South Carolina. Greene had liberated the backcountry of both states, and the British now clung only to Savannah and Charles Town.

With his own army battered and bleeding and lacking siege weapons, General Greene had to pull back to a rest camp on the High Hills of the Santee to nurse his army's wounds and await reinforcements. Then in November he moved his revived force closer to Charles Town; he ordered General Thomas Sumter to move east from Orangeburg while General Francis Marion established a headquarters at Monck's Corner. The proverbial shoe was now on the other foot. The British garrison faced encirclement.

Patriot soldiers and civilians in South Carolina were cheered by the news from York Town, Virginia, in the fall when, in General Greene's words, "the old fox got into the trap at last." But reports reaching Charles Town of the surrender of Lord Cornwallis' army of 8,000 quite shattered the morale of the British troops and Loyalists. When news of the defeat reached London, it shattered the last British hopes for a victory in America. It led to the collapse of Lord North's ministry and to the opening of peace negotiations. But while politicians dickered over a settlement in Europe and troops stacked arms elsewhere in America, the war dragged on in lowcountry South Carolina.

In January, 1782, General Greene moved his army near Jacksonborough, about 30 miles from Charles Town, to protect representatives from across the state attending the first meeting of the state legislature in several years. Governor John Rutledge's rolling coach, so long the seat of the Patriot government of South Carolina, was nearing the end of its journey.

A spirit of vindictiveness pervaded the meeting. Many of the lowcountry elite desired retribution. A member of the Assembly wrote that an "inveterate hatred & spirit of vengeance" prevails; "the very females talk as familiarly of sheding blood & destroying the [Loyalists] as the men do." An "enemies list" mentality was emerging. The names of those Charles Town citizens who had addressed petitions to Clinton and Cornwallis several years before were among the first to appear on lists drawn up by the legislators. Identified as Loyalists, they were to be banished from the state and their property confiscated or amerced. A total of 146 citizens of Charles Town were affected by the acts.

After the Confiscation Bill passed the Legislature and General Greene's army moved closer to Charles Town, reports from within indicated that civilian Loyalists were beginning to "sweat." They had suddenly "lost their spirit and their hopes." Patriot prisoners in the garrisoned town were "treated with every affection of civility & they deign to call them Americans." And with the changing of the tide of war at Charles Town, some zealous Loyalists were now avowing that they had always been zealous "rebels." Loyalist refugees from the town began flocking into the American lines.

Besides wanting to join the "right" side, Loyalists were coming into Greene's army because of severe food shortages in Charles Town. One resident attempted to make light of a situation growing more acute each day. He sent out a plea to General Greene in the form of a poem. It read:

Since we have but little here to eat
Have sent you my knives to carve your meat
Whither they be good or not
They are the Best that I have got

If my request your favour meet
Send some Cattle on their feet —
Whither they be wild or tame
I'll pay the owners for the same

Little did the would-be poet know that shortages of beef within Greene's army were equally severe. The army was so short on meat that cattle were slaughtered before they fattened. An account by one of Greene's soldiers illustrates these conditions. As the soldier returned from the slaughtering pens one morning, a comrade-in-arms asked him how the cattle were faring. He replied "that it took two men to hold up a creature until the butcher knocked it down." On hearing this, his comrade-in-arms asked: "Why didn't he knock it down as it lay?"

Still without siege weapons, reinforcements, and supplies, his troops suffering from lowcountry fevers, Greene stationed his army along the western bank of the Ashley where they waited and watched Charles Town during the spring and summer. In early August, 1782, General Alexander Leslie, now commander of the British garrison, received orders from London to evacuate the town. A few weeks later the beloved son of Henry Laurens, young Colonel John Laurens, was shot and killed in an ambush while leading a 50-man force tracking a British foraging party near Combahee Ferry. A member of the lowcountry elite and a man of great promise, he died needlessly in the last months of the war. Even some Loyalists bemoaned the loss. The British-controlled Charles Town press eulogized him and hoped that another young "Laurens could be found!"

The news that the British planned to evacuate the city quickly spread across the lowcountry. In great anticipation Patriot South Carolinians awaited the departure of the British; Charles Town natives eagerly looked forward to returning home to hearth, family, and friends. Rumors flew. When Edward Rutledge heard that the British planned to burn the town upon embarkation, he vowed "to God" to seek retaliation by "setting fire to the

Colonel John Laurens
(ambushed and killed near Combahee Ferry, August 1782)

city of London." Long separated by just a few British-occupied miles from the woman he loved, Colonel Lewis Morris of Greene's army wrote Miss Ann Elliott at Charles Town in the late summer: "Never, never will I suffer the pang of such another separation."

By the early fall negotiations were completed between the opposing generals, Leslie and Greene, on the procedures for the evacuation. The British agreed to leave the city in good order on the condition that Greene's forces not attack during embarkation. In mid-November a secret report sent to Greene's headquarters from inside the town revealed that the departure date for the British was near. The intelligence report stated that "the town is in the greatest confusion; the removal of household furniture, merchandise" is going apace and "great dispatch is used in getting the fleet ready."

Learning of this report, Colonel Morris in great delight wrote Miss Elliott on November 28: "I amuse myself with the pleasing fond expectation of seeing you the next week. Everybody agrees the British will embark." But a few days later he lamented, "December has arrived and the enemy are yet in Charles Town. I am still, my dearest girl, hanging upon the thread of suspense." But on December 13 Lewis' hopes surged and he wrote Ann: "Our prospects brighten, my spirits revive. Oh my soul! I am told the fleet is in motion." So eager to see her, he wrote: "Good God my heart can scarcely contain itself for joy!" That same day and the next, British troops, South Carolina Loyalists, and their slaves embarked. Nearly 10,000 persons departed Charles Town.

In the early morning chill of December 14 a British officer embarking troops at Christopher Gadsden's wharf on the Cooper detected "gloomy despair" on the faces of civilian Loyalists as he watched one British regiment after another file aboard the waiting transports. About midmorning, after the firing of a single signal cannon, a war-weary American force under General "Mad Anthony" Wayne, stepping to martial tunes, their tattered banners fluttering, marched through the town gates. They closed on the rear guard of General Leslie's army marching down King Street to the sounds of fife and drum. Some of the troops exchanged greetings; several British officers shouted that the Americans were closing too fast.

By midafternoon the chill that had hung over the town at dawn was nearly gone. About 3 o'clock General Greene, General Moultrie, newly-elected Governor John Mathews, and their wives riding near them in carriages led a column of Continentals down Broad Street. Behind the troops poured a flock of camp followers. The procession halted before the State House, and General Greene escorted the governor inside. American government was being restored to town and state at the same time the royal government was departing for the last time.

In the harbor dozens of ships were unreefing their topsails, and British sea captains were charting their courses across the bar and into the open ocean to Jamaica, Florida, England, or St. Lucia. It was a time for the pealing of bells, but no sounds came from the steeple of St. Michael's. Along with other private and public plunder, the bells were bound for England. No matter, it was a day long awaited by some though dreaded by others. Celebrations soon began.

Perhaps there was no man happier in Charles Town on that December 14, 1782, than General Moultrie. As a

Courtesy Museum of Early Southern Decorative Arts

Charles Town Harbor Where the British Fleet Departed
December 14, 1782

prisoner of the British, he had been cooped up in the town for over two years. Personally, he had reason to mean it when he said that for Carolinians "it was the real day of their deliverance and independence." Ringing in his ears down through the years were the congratulations and praises heaped on the American troops that day by young and old alike: "God bless you, gentlemen! You are welcome home gentlemen!"

Bibliography

ARTICLES

Andreano, Ralph Louis, and Herbert D. Werner. "Charleston Loyalists: A Statistical Note," *South Carolina Historical Magazine* (July, 1959).

"Autobiography of Daniel Stevens, 1746-1835" *South Carolina Historical Magazine* (January, 1957).

Bargar, B. D. "Charles Town Loyalism in 1775: The Secret Reports of Alexander Innes," *South Carolina Historical Magazine* (July, 1962).

Barnwell, Joseph W. "The Evacuation of Charleston by the British in 1782," *The South Carolina Historical and Genealogical Magazine* (January, 1910).

_____. "Letters to General Greene and Others," *The South Carolina Historical and Genealogical Magazine* (January, 1916).

_____. "Letters to General Greene and Others," *The South Carolina Historical and Genealogical Magazine* (April, 1916).

_____. "Letters of John Rutledge," *The South Carolina Historical and Genealogical Magazine* (October, 1916).

_____. "Letters of John Rutledge," *The South Carolina Historical and Genealogical Magazine* (October, 1917).

_____. "Hon. Charles Garth, M.P., The Last Colonial Agent of South Carolina in England, and Some of His Work," *The South Carolina Historical and Genealogical Magazine* (April, 1925).

_____. "Correspondence of Hon. Arthur Middleton, Signer of the Declaration of Independence," *The South Carolina Historical and Genealogical Magazine* (October, 1925).

_____. "Correspondence of Hon. Arthur Middleton," *The South Carolina Historical and Genealogical Magazine* (July, 1926).

_____. "Correspondence of Charles Garth: The Pitt Statue," *The South Carolina Historical and Genealogical Magazine* (April, 1927).

Barnwell, Robert W., Jr. "The Migration of Loyalists From South Carolina," *The Proceedings of the South Carolina Historical Association* (1937).

Baskett, Sam S. "Eliza Lucas Pinckney: Portrait of an Eighteenth

Century American," *South Carolina Historical Magazine* (October, 1971).

Bennett, John. "A List of Noncommissioned Officers and Private Men of the Second South Carolina Continental Regiment of Foot," *The South Carolina Historical and Genealogical Magazine* (January, 1915).

_____. "The Marion-Gadsden Correspondence," *The South Carolina Historical and Genealogical Magazine* (April, 1940).

_____. "Charleston in 1774 as Described by an English Traveler," *The South Carolina Historical and Genealogical Magazine* (July, 1946).

Brown, Alan S. "James Simpson's Reports on the Carolina Loyalists, 1779-1780," *The Journal of Southern History* (November, 1955).

Bulger, William T. "Sir Henry Clinton's 'Journal of the Siege of Charleston, 1780,'" *South Carolina Historical Magazine* (July, 1965).

Bull, Henry DeSaussure. "Ashley Hall Plantation," *The South Carolina Historical and Genealogical Magazine* (April, 1952).

Calhoun, Robert M., and Robert H. Weir. "'The Scandalous History of Sir Egerton Leigh,'" *William and Mary Quarterly* (January, 1969).

"The Case of The General's Dog," *American Heritage* (June, 1964).

Cohen, Hennig. "Four Letters from Peter Timothy, 1755, 1768, 1771," *South Carolina Historical Magazine* (July, 1954).

Cross, Jack L. "Letters of Thomas Pinckney, 1775-1780," *South Carolina Historical Magazine* (January, April, July, October, 1957).

Crouse, Maurice A. "Papers of Gabriel Manigault, 1771-1784," *South Carolina Historical Magazine* (January, 1963).

_____. "Gabriel Manigault: Charleston Merchant," *South Carolina Historical Magazine* (October, 1967).

_____. "The Letterbook of Peter Manigault, 1763-1773," *South Carolina Historical Magazine* (April, 1969).

_____. "Cautious Rebellion: South Carolina's Opposition to the Stamp Act," *South Carolina Historical Magazine* (April, 1972).

Curtis, Mary Julia. "Charles-Town's Church Street Theater," *South Carolina Historical Magazine* (July, 1969).

Dabney, William M. "Drayton and Laurens in the Continental

Congress," *South Carolina Historical Magazine* (April, 1959).

"Diary of Captain Barnard Elliott," *Year Book City of Charleston, 1899* (Charleston, 1899).

Duffy, John. "Yellow Fever in Colonial Charleston," *The South Carolina Historical and Genealogical Magazine* (October, 1951).

Easterby, J. H. "Public Poor Relief in Colonial Charleston," *The South Carolina Historical and Genealogical Magazine* (April, 1940).

Farley, Foster M. "The South Carolina Negro in the American Revolution, 1775-1783," *South Carolina Historical Magazine* (April, 1978).

Fenhagen, Mary Pringle. "Letters and Will of Robert Pringle (1702-1776)," *The South Carolina Historical and Genealogical Magazine* (July, 1949).

Fraser, Walter J., Jr. "Tea, Taxes, and Temerity: A Meeting at the Exchange Building, December 3, 1773" (Charleston, 1973).

_____. "Reflections of 'Democracy' in Revolutionary South Carolina? The Composition of Military Organizations and the Attitudes and Relationships of the Officers and Men, 1775-1780," *South Carolina Historical Magazine* (July, 1977).

_____. "Controlling the Poor in Colonial Charles Town," *Proceedings of the South Carolina Historical Association* (1980).

_____. "The City Elite, 'Disorder,' and the Poor Children of Pre-Revolutionary Charleston," *South Carolina Historical Magazine* (July, 1983).

Gayle, Charles Joseph. "The Nature and Volume of Exports from Charleston," *The Proceedings of the South Carolina Historical Association* (1937).

Greene, Jack P. "The South Carolina Quartering Dispute, 1757-1758," *South Carolina Historical Magazine* (October, 1959).

_____. "The Gadsden Election Controversy and the Revolutionary Movement in South Carolina," *Mississippi Valley Historical Review* (December, 1959).

_____. "The Role of the Lower Houses of Assembly in Eighteenth-Century Politics," *The Journal of Southern History* (November, 1961).

_____. "The Political Authorship of Sir Egerton Leigh," *South Carolina Historical Magazine* (July, 1974).

_____. "'Slavery or Independence': Some Reflections on the Relationship among Liberty, Black Bondage, and Equality in

Revolutionary South Carolina," *South Carolina Historical Magazine* (July, 1979).

Harrigan, Anthony. "The Charleston Tradition," *American Heritage* (February, 1958).

Haywood, C. Robert. "Mercantilism and South Carolina Agriculture, 1700-1763," *South Carolina Historical Magazine* (January, 1959).

Higgins, W. Robert. "Charles Town Merchants and Factors Dealing in the External Negro Trade, 1735-1775," *South Carolina Historical Magazine* (October, 1964).

_____. "The South Carolina Revolutionary Debt and Its Holders, 1776-1780," *South Carolina Historical Magazine* (January, 1971).

Hubbell, Jay B. "'On Liberty-Tree:' A Revolutionary Poem from South Carolina," *The South Carolina Historical and Genealogical Magazine* (July, 1940).

Jervey, Theodore D. "Reverend Robert Cooper," *The South Carolina Historical and Genealogical Magazine* (October, 1937).

Jones, Newton B. "Writings of the Reverend William Tennent, 1740-1777," *South Carolina Historical Magazine* (July, 1960).

"Journal of the Second Council of Safety," *Collections of the South Carolina Historical Society* (Charleston, 1859).

Kepner, Frances Reece. "A British View of the Siege of Charleston, 1776," *Journal of Southern History* (February, 1945).

Kyte, George W. "General Greene's Plans for the Capture of Charleston, 1781-1782," *South Carolina Historical Magazine* (April, 1961).

"Letter from John Laurens to his Uncle James Laurens," *South Carolina Historical Magazine* (January, 1909).

"Letters of General Francis Marion," *Year Book City of Charleston, 1895* (Charleston, 1895).

"Letters from Hon. Henry Laurens to his Son John, 1773-1776," *The South Carolina Historical and Genealogical Magazine* (July, 1904).

"Letters of Gen. Francis Marion," *Year Book City of Charleston, 1895* (Charleston, 1895).

Levett, Ella Pettit. "Loyalism in Charleston, 1761-1784." *Proceedings of the South Carolina Historical Association* (1936).

Maier, Pauline. "The Charleston Mob and the Evolution of Popular Politics in Revolutionary South Carolina, 1765-1784," *Perspectives in American History* (1970).

Maslowski, Pete. "National Policy Toward the Use of Black Troops in The Revolution," *South Carolina Historical Magazine* (January, 1972).

Merrens, H. Roy. "A View of Coastal South Carolina in 1778: The Journal of Ebenezer Hazard," *South Carolina Historical Magazine* (October, 1972).

Minchinton, Walter E. "Richard Champion, Nicholas Pocock, and the Carolina Trade: A Note," *South Carolina Historical Magazine* (April, 1969).

_____. "Richard Champion, Nicholas Pocock, and the Carolina Trade," *South Carolina Historical Magazine* (April, 1964).

"Miscellaneous Papers of the General Committee and Provincial Congress, 1775," *The South Carolina Historical and Genealogical Magazine* (July, 1907, 1908).

Mouzon, Harold A. "The Ship 'Prosper,' 1775-1776," *South Carolina Historical Magazine* (January, 1958).

Murdoch, Richard K. "A French Account of the Siege of Charleston, 1780," *South Carolina Historical Magazine* (July, 1966).

Myers, T. Bailey. "Original Letters 1775-1789 Period," *Year Book City of Charleston, 1882* (Charleston, 1882).

Olsberg, R. Nicholas. "Ship Registers in the South Carolina Archives, 1734-1780," *South Carolina Historical Magazine* (October, 1973).

Olson, Gary D. "Loyalists and the American Revolution: Thomas Brown and the South Carolina Backcountry, 1775-1776," *South Carolina Historical Magazine* (October, 1967).

Olwell, Robert A. "'Domestick Enemies': Slavery and Political Independence in South Carolina, May 1775-March 1776," *Journal of Southern History* (February, 1989).

"Order Book of John Faucheraud Grimke," *The South Carolina Historical and Genealogical Magazine* (April, 1912, July, 1916, October, 1917, April, 1918, October, 1918).

"Order Book of the 1st Regt., S.C. Line, Continental Establishment," *The South Carolina Historical and Genealogical Magazine* (July, 1906, April, 1907).

"Papers of the First Council of Safety of the Revolutionary Party of S.C.," *The South Carolina Historical and Genealogical Magazine* (October, 1900).

Richardson, Emma B. "Letters of William Richardson, 1765-1784," *The South Carolina Historical and Genealogical Magazine* (January, 1946).

Rogers, George C., Jr. "Aedanus Burke, Nathanael Greene, Anthony Wayne, and the British Merchants of Charleston," *South Carolina Historical Magazine* (April, 1966).

_____. "The Charleston Tea Party: The Significance of December 3, 1773," *South Carolina Historical Magazine* (July, 1974).

Ryan, Frank Winkler, Jr. "Travelers in South Carolina in the Eighteenth Century," *Year Book City of Charleston, S.C., 1945* (Charleston, 1945).

_____. "The Role of South Carolina in the First Continental Congress," *South Carolina Historical Magazine* (July, 1959).

Salley, A. S. "Diary of William Dillwyn During a Visit to Charles Town in 1772," *The South Carolina Historical and Genealogical Magazine* (January, 1935).

Sharrer, G. Terry. "Indigo in Carolina, 1671-1796," *South Carolina Historical Magazine* (April, 1971).

"Siege of Charleston: Journal of Captain Peter Russell, December 25, 1779, to May 2, 1780," *American Historical Review* (April, 1899).

Sifton, Paul G. "La Caroline Meridionale: Some French Sources of South Carolina Revolutionary History, with Two Unpublished Letters of Baron de Kalb," *South Carolina Historical Magazine* (April, 1965).

Simons, Harriett P., and Albert Simons. "The William Burrows House of Charleston," *South Carolina Historical Magazine* (July, 1969).

Simons, Robert B. "Regimental Book of Captain James Bentham, 1778-1780," *The South Carolina Historical and Genealogical Magazine* (January, 1952).

Smith, D. E. Huger. "Commodore Alexander Gillon and the Frigate South Carolina," *The South Carolina Historical and Genealogical Magazine* (October, 1908).

_____. "Wilton's Statue of Pitt," *The South Carolina Historical and Genealogical Magazine* (January, 1914).

_____. "Nisbett of Dean and Dean Hall," *The South Carolina Historical and Genealogical Magazine* (January, April, 1923).

_____. "Letters from Col. Lewis Morris to Miss Ann Elliott," *The South Carolina Historical and Genealogical Magazine* (October, 1939, January, 1940).

Smith, J. J. Pringle. "Sketch of the History of Charleston, S.C.," *Year Book City of Charleston, S.C., 1880* (Charleston, 1880).

_____. "The Government of the City of Charleston, 1682-

1882," *Year Book City of Charleston, S.C., 1881* (Charleston, 1881).

Smith, Henry A. N. "Charleston and Charleston Neck: The Original Grantees and the Settlements Along the Ashley and Cooper Rivers," *The South Carolina Historical and Genealogical Magazine* (January, 1918).

_____. "The Ashley River: Its Seats and Settlements," *The South Carolina Historical and Genealogical Magazine* (January, April, 1919).

Starr. Raymond. "Letters from John Lewis Gervais to Henry Laurens, 1777-1778," *South Carolina Historical Magazine* (January, 1965).

Steedman, Marguerite. "Charlestown's Forgotten Tea Party," *The Georgia Review* (Summer, 1967).

_____. "Susannah Elliott's Blue Flag Comes Home," *South Carolina History Illustrated* (November, 1970).

Stoesen, Alexander R. "The British Occupation of Charleston, 1780-1782," *South Carolina Historical Magazine* (April, 1962).

Stokes, Durward T. "The Presbyterian Clergy in South Carolina and the American Revolution," *South Carolina Historical Magazine* (October, 1970).

_____. "The Baptist and Methodist Clergy in South Carolina and the American Revolution," *South Carolina Historical Magazine* (April, 1972).

Tobias, Thomas J. "Charles Town in 1764," *South Carolina Historical Magazine* (April, 1966).

Ulmer, S. Sidney. "Some Eighteenth Century South Carolinians and the Duel," *South Carolina Historical Magazine* (January, 1959).

Ver Steeg, Clarence L. "Stacey Hepburn and Company: Enterprisers in the American Revolution," *South Carolina Historical Magazine* (January, 1954).

Villers, David H. "The Smythe Horses Affair and the Association," *South Carolina Historical Magazine* (July, 1969).

Walsh, Walter Richard. "Edmund Egan: Charleston's Rebel Brewer," *South Carolina Historical Magazine* (October, 1955).

_____. "The Charleston Mechanics: A Brief Study, 1760-1776," *South Carolina Historical Magazine* (July, 1959).

_____. "Christopher Gadsden: Radical or Conservative Revolutionary?," *South Carolina Historical Magazine* (July, 1962).

Way, William Rev. "The Old Exchange and Custom House," (Charleston, 1921).

Webber, Mabel L. "Death Notices from the South Carolina and American General Gazette, and its Continuation the Royal Gazette," *The South Carolina Historical and Genealogical Magazine* (October, 1915).

_____. "Extracts from the Journal of Mrs. Ann Manigault," *The South Carolina Historical and Genealogical Magazine* (April, July, 1919, July, 1920).

_____. "Josiah Smith's Diary, 1780-1781," *The South Carolina Historical and Genealogical Magazine* (January, 1932).

_____. "Revolutionary Letters," *The South Carolina Historical and Genealogical Magazine* (January, 1937).

Weir, Robert M. "'The Harmony We Were Famous For': An Interpretation of Pre-Revolutionary South Carolina Politics," *William and Mary Quarterly* (October, 1969).

_____. "Two Letters by Christopher Gadsden, February 1766," *South Carolina Historical Magazine* (July, 1974).

_____. "'The Violent Spirit,' the Reestablishment of Order, and the Continuity of Leadership in Post-Revolutionary South Carolina." In *An Uncivil War: The Southern Backcountry during the American Revolution*, eds. Ronald Hoffman, et al. Charlottesville: The University Press of Virginia, 1985.

Whilden, William G. "Diary of the Rev. Oliver Hart," *Year Book City of Charleston, S.C., 1896* (Charleston, 1896).

Wood, Peter H. "'Taking Care of Business' in Revolutionary South Carolina: Republicanism and the Slave Society." In *South Atlantic Urban Studies*, ed. Jack R. Censer. Columbia: University of South Carolina Press, 1978.

Woody, Robert H. "Christopher Gadsden and the Stamp Act," *Proceedings of the South Carolina Historical Association* (1939).

BOOKS

Alden, John R. *A History of the American Revolution.* New York: Knopf, 1969.

_____. *The South in the Revolution, 1763-1789.* Baton Rouge: Louisiana State University Press, 1957.

_____. *General Charles Lee: Traitor or Patriot?* Baton Rouge: Louisiana State University Press, 1951.

Berkeley, Edmund, and Dorothy Smith Berkeley. *Dr. Alexander*

Garden of Charles Town. Chapel Hill: University of North Carolina Press, 1969.

Bowen, David K. *The Execution of Isaac Hayne.* Lexington, South Carolina: Sandlapper Press, 1977.

Bowes, Frederick P. *The Culture of Early Charleston.* Chapel Hill: University of North Carolina Press, 1942.

Bridenbaugh, Carl. *Myths and Realities: Societies of the Colonial South.* Baton Rouge: Louisiana State University Press, 1952.

_____. *Cities in Revolt: Urban Life in America, 1743-1776.* New York: Capricorn Books, 1964.

Brown, Wallace. *The King's Friends: The Composition and Motives of the American Loyalist Claimants.* Providence: Brown University Press, 1965.

Bull, Kinloch, Jr. *The Oligarchs in Colonial and Revolutionary Charleston: Lieutenant Governor William Bull II and His Family.* Columbia: University of South Carolina Press, 1991.

Burton, E. Milby. *Charleston Furniture, 1700-1825.* Charleston: The Charleston Museum, 1955.

Cohen, Hennig. *The South Carolina Gazette, 1732-1775.* Columbia: University of South Carolina Press, 1953.

Davidson, Chalmers G. *Friend of the People: The Life of Dr. Peter Fayssoux.* Columbia: The Medical Association of South Carolina, 1950.

Drayton, John. *Memoirs of the American Revolution.* 2 vols. Charleston: A. E. Miller, 1821.

Fraser, Walter J., Jr. *Charleston! Charleston!: The History of a Southern City.* Columbia: University of South Carolina Press, 1989.

Frey, Sylvia R. *Water from the Rock: Black Resistance in a Revolutionary Age.* Princeton: Princeton University Press, 1991.

Garden, Alexander. *Anecdotes of the Revolutionary War in America.* Charleston: A. E. Miller, 1822.

Godbold, E. Stanly, Jr., and Robert H. Woody. *Christopher Gadsden and the American Revolution.* Knoxville: University of Tennessee Press, 1982.

Greene, Jack P. *The Quest for Power: The Lower Houses of Assembly in the Southern Royal Colonies, 1689-1776.* Chapel Hill: University of North Carolina Press, 1963.

_____. *The Nature of Colony Constitutions: Two Pamphlets on the Wilkes Fund Controversy in South Carolina.* Columbia: University of South Carolina Press, 1970.

Gregorie, Anne King. *Thomas Sumter.* Columbia: The R. L. Bryan Company, 1931.

Hamer, Philip M., and George C. Rogers, Jr. *The Papers of Henry Laurens, September 11, 1746-October 31, 1755.* Columbia: University of South Carolina Press, 1968.

Higginbotham, Don. *The War of American Independence: Military Attitudes, Policies, and Practice, 1763-1789.* New York: The Macmillan Company, 1971.

Johnson, Joseph. *Traditions and Reminiscences Chiefly of the American Revolution in the South.* Charleston: Walker & James, 1851.

Jordan, Winthrop D. *White Over Black: American Attitudes Toward the Negro, 1550-1812.* Chapel Hill: University of North Carolina Press, 1968.

Lambert, Robert S. *South Carolina Loyalists in the American Revolution.* Columbia: University of South Carolina Press, 1987.

McCowen, George Smith, Jr. *The British Occupation of Charleston, 1780-1782.* Columbia: University of South Carolina Press, 1972.

McCrady, Edward. *The History of South Carolina Under the Royal Government, 1719-1776.* New York: Macmillan, 1899.

_____. *South Carolina in the Revolution, 1775-1780.* New York: Macmillan, 1901.

_____. *South Carolina in the Revolution, 1780-1783.* New York: Macmillan, 1902.

McMaster, Fitzhugh. *Soldiers and Uniforms: South Carolina Military Affairs, 1670-1775.* Columbia: University of South Carolina Press, 1971.

Nadelhaft, Jerome J. *The Disorders of War: The Revolution in South Carolina.* Orono: University of Orono at Maine Press, 1981.

Nevins, Allan. *The American States During and After the Revolution, 1775-1789.* New York: The Macmillan Company, 1927.

Quarles, Benjamin. *The Negro in the American Revolution.* Chapel Hill: University of North Carolina Press, 1961.

Rankin, Hugh F. *The Theater in Colonial America.* Chapel Hill: University of North Carolina Press, 1965.

Ravenel, Harriott Horry. *Eliza Pinckney.* New York: Scribner's Sons, 1896.

Ravenel, Mrs. St. Julien. *Charleston: The Place and the People.* New York: Macmillan, 1906.

Rogers, George C., Jr. *Charleston in the Age of the Pinckneys.* Norman: University of Oklahoma Press, 1969.

Shaffer, Arthur H. *To Be An American: David Ramsay and the*

Making of the American Consciousness. Columbia: University of South Carolina Press, 1991.

Sellers, Leila. *Charleston Business on the Eve of the American Revolution.* Chapel Hill: University of North Carolina Press, 1934.

Sirmans, M. Eugene. *Colonial South Carolina: A Political History, 1663-1763.* Chapel Hill: University of North Carolina Press, 1966.

Smith, Warren B. *White Servitude in Colonial South Carolina.* Columbia: University of South Carolina Press, 1961.

Spruill, Julia Cherry. *Women's Life and Work in the Southern Colonies.* Chapel Hill: University of North Carolina Press, 1938.

Thayer, Theodore. *Nathanael Greene: Strategist of the American Revolution.* New York: Twayne Publishers, 1960.

Uhlendorf, Bernhard A. *The Siege of Charleston.* Ann Arbor: University of Michigan Press, 1938.

Vipperman, Carl J. *The Rise of Rawlins Lowndes, 1721-1800.* Columbia: University of South Carolina Press, 1978.

Wallace, David D. *The Life of Henry Laurens.* New York: Putnam, 1915.

_____. *South Carolina, A Short History, 1520-1948.* Columbia: University of South Carolina Press, 1969.

Wallace, Willard. *Appeal to Arms: A Military History of the American Revolution.* New York: Harper and Row, 1951.

Walsh, Richard. *Charleston's Sons of Liberty: A Study of the Artisans, 1763-1789.* Columbia: University of South Carolina Press, 1966.

_____. *The Writings of Christopher Gadsden, 1746-1805.* Columbia: University of South Carolina Press, 1966.

Waring, Joseph I. *A History of Medicine in South Carolina, 1670-1825.* Columbia: The R. L. Bryan Company, 1964.

Weigley, Russell F. *The Partisan War: The South Carolina Campaign of 1780-1782.* Columbia: University of South Carolina Press, 1970.

Weir, Robert M. *"A Most Important Epocha:" The Coming of the Revolution in South Carolina.* Columbia: University of South Carolina Press, 1970.

_____. *Colonial South Carolina: A History.* Millwood, New York: KTO Press, 1983.

Willcox, William B. *The American Rebellion: Sir Henry Clinton's Narrative of his Campaigns, 1775-1782.* Hamden, Connecticut: The Shoe String Press, Inc., 1971.

_____. *Portrait of A General: Sir Henry Clinton in the War of Independence.* New York: Knopf, 1964.

Williams, George W. *St. Michael's Charleston, 1751-1951.* Columbia: University of South Carolina Press, 1951.

Zahniser, Marvin R. *Charles Cotesworth Pinckney: Founding Father.* Chapel Hill: University of North Carolina Press, 1967.

DISSERTATIONS

Cavanagh, John Carroll. "The Military Career of Major General Benjamin Lincoln in the War of the American Revolution, 1775-1781." Ph.D. dissertation, Duke University, 1969.

Clow, Brent. "Edward Rutledge of South Carolina, 1749-1800: Unproclaimed Statesman." Ph.D. dissertation, University of Georgia, 1976.

Starr, Raymond G. "The Conservative Revolution: South Carolina Public Affairs, 1775-1790." Ph.D. dissertation, University of Texas, 1964.

NEWSPAPERS

South Carolina Gazette
South Carolina Gazette and Country Journal
South Carolina General and American Gazette